Happier Than A Billionaire:

Picking a Town
Finding a Home
and
Creating a Budget in Costa Rica

by Nadine Hays Pisani

Happier Than A Billionaire: Picking a Town, Finding a Home, and Creating a Budget in Costa Rica
2019 / Nadine Hays Pisani -- 1st ed.
ISBN: 9781698057125

Dedication

To the readers, for whose support I will always be grateful.

Books

- *Happier Than A Billionaire: Quitting My Job, Moving to Costa Rica, & Living the Zero Hour Work Week*
- *Happier Than A Billionaire: The Sequel*
- *Happier Than A Billionaire: An Acre in Paradise*
- *The Costa Rica Escape Manual* 2014, 2016, 2019

Connect with Me

- www.facebook.com/happierthanabillionaire
- www.happierthanabillionaire.com
- www.instagram.com/happierthanabillionaire
- www.youtube.com/happierthanabillionaire
- www.twitter.com/happierwithless

email: puravida@happierthanabillionaire.com

Contents

Picking a Town

Finding A Home

Creating a Budget

Real People with Real Budgets

Bonus Chapter from
The Costa Rica Escape Manual 2019

Acknowledgments

I could not have completed this book without the help and support of my husband, Rob. Thank you for giving me the space to write. It's the only thing I've ever wanted to do.

Thank you to my mother and father who taught me to work hard. I hope you return to Costa Rica and pick some of Rob's plantains. Or they may be bananas. I have problems distinguishing between the two.

And a big thank you to everyone off Exit 13 in New Jersey. Don't let the oil refinery fool you. There is a big heart in that industrial town.

"I felt my lungs inflate with the onrush of
scenery—air, mountains, trees, people. I thought,
"This is what it is to be happy."

~Sylvia Plath

Map

Where Do I Begin

Never forget, today, you have 100% of your life left.
~ Tom Hopkins

You're watching a house hunting show about a couple that moved to Costa Rica. They purchased an ocean-view home surrounded by fruit trees and howler monkeys, and now you're curious. You daydream about the possibilities of this exotic life.

"Wouldn't it be nice to skip out on the rat race for a while?" you ask yourself. If something is drawing you to this beautiful country, you're not alone.

Many of us long for a new start, while others desire a life less ordinary. Some of us have an internal compass that keeps spinning. We dream of going east to explore ancient ruins or south for more sunshine, and this magnetic pull makes it difficult to stay in one place.

The people you watched on that house hunting show may have been my husband, Rob, and I: The Happier Couple. Our compass pulled us away from steady jobs in the United States to a very unsteady adventure in a foreign country. It's been a crazy ride, but we've never looked back. A wild, bumpy dirt road guides us toward new places creating, exciting stories to tell. Today we run The Happier House and host guests looking to relocate to Costa Rica.

The scope of this book is limited when compared to my others. It can only point you in three directions: picking a town, finding a home, and creating a budget answering the most frequent question I get asked:

How do I find a place to live on a budget that's right for me?

This book explores several factors, including the type of homes you might find in popular areas around the country and what they might cost in each. It'll focus on picking a town, finding a home, and creating a budget. None of these components is more important than the other. They can be used together in order to help you find the right home in the right town for you.

Picking a Town

We'll travel throughout the country and compare lifestyle and cost throughout the Central Valley, Guanacaste Province, the southern Pacific coast, and the Caribbean. I'll discuss the differences in weather, healthcare, utilities, and proximity to the nearest international airport.

I've chosen a handful of popular towns from each area, but that isn't meant to dissuade you from considering other spots. My selections are meant as a good starting point for your house hunting search.

Finding a Home

It's fun to imagine living off the grid in a tree house. But how far is the grocery store? Is there a gas station in the area? An MRI machine in case you fall out of that tree house? Some people may want to be close to amenities while others are willing to travel when necessary.

"I don't mind living far from town, but will I have to drive through a creek to get to my house?" you ask the realtor. The answer could be yes if you're looking for a bargain. And that creek will most likely turn into a river in the rainy season.

You'll notice some people have a snorkel on their vehicle. This is a pipe attached to the carburetor that extends over the roof, which prevents the motor from stalling while driving through high waters. You may think it's because they enjoy off-roading, but every day is off-roading in some parts of this country. My husband and I like to stay on-roading as often as possible.

Major Topics in "Finding a Home" include:

Housing Styles: I've broken down housing styles into three categories. What's a Tico-style home? What is the difference between moderately appointed and gringo style? There is a correlation between price and each housing style.

Renting on Three Different Monthly Budgets: We'll explore three monthly budgets that often correlate with my three categories of homes: $1200/month, $2500/month, and $3500/month. This amount represents not just rent, but your entire monthly budget, including groceries, healthcare, utilities, etc.

Searching for Listings: Where do I start to look for housing? I'll point to some of the best places to begin your search.

Different Strokes: What are suicide showers? Why can't I flush my toilet paper? Why are there bars on the windows? We'll cover that and more so you'll know what to expect.

Timing of Your Move: Thinking about finding a long-term rental starting mid-December? You don't want to skip the chapter "When to Rent: The Christmas & Easter Conundrum."

Buying a Piece of Land: Are you buying a piece of land and leaving it unattended for a while? Have you heard of squatters' rights? I'll explain how to avoid this prickly situation and your legal recourse.

Buying a Beachfront Home: Is the house 50 meters from the water's edge at high tide? I'll break down Maritime Zone regulations and discuss how they affect the title of a home.

Purchasing Real Estate: Are you dreaming of owning a home near a babbling brook? How about a condominium overlooking the Pacific Ocean? We will explore five price categories and what types of homes you might find for the money.

- Under $150,000
- $150,000-$250,000
- $250,000-$375,000
- $375,000-$500,000
- Over $500,000

Creating a Budget

Once you've reviewed the tools I prepared, you'll be ready to pick a town, find a home, and create a budget. I'll assume you have a stable income and are not sending your children to private school. If you need more information on these topics and others, I refer you to *The Costa Rica Escape Manual 2019.*

Once you choose a suitable housing category—Tico, moderately appointed, or gringo style—in a town you love, you can review the sample listings I provided. You will then be able to place yourself in one of the following monthly budgets: $1200/month, $2500/month, and $3500/month.

For $1200 and $2500 monthly budgets, we'll allocate approximately 35% toward rent. But for the monthly budget of $3500, I'm upping that number to 45%. The place where you live is a big part of your lifestyle, and this is where I would splurge. An incredible view of the Central Valley, combined with a backyard filled with fruit trees, is a cure for the tired soul. But you don't necessarily have to be on a higher budget to find that. It's surprising how great some rentals can be if you're willing to sacrifice some things we normally take for granted.

Major Topics in "Creating a Budget" include:

The Four Budget Breakers: Before creating a budget, you'll want to dive into this chapter and answer yes or no to four questions. How you answer may determine whether or not you can afford to live in Costa Rica.

Lifestyle: Are there items you can live without? What sacrifices are you willing to make?

Real People with Real Budgets: We will meet real people from around the country. Some own their houses while others rent. We'll break their expenses down into the following categories: **automobile, home, utilities, entertainment, groceries, pets, and medical.** They'll even share tips on how to save money, traps to avoid, and ways to stretch a buck.

Don't be disappointed if your budget doesn't fulfill all of your dreams. Some of the happiest people I've ever met were surfers bunking together in a van. They find ways to earn a modest living and continue doing what they love most—more surfing. Is there a passion in your life worth exploring? Would you trade in sixty-hour work weeks for something that allows more time to play your guitar? Once you meet a happy surfer, it makes you reconsider many of your priorities.

Included Chapters from the latest edition of
The Costa Rica Escape Manual 2019

There's a lot to understand about choosing a home in Costa Rica. You need to be aware of many things unique to this country. To make sure you have as much information on hand, I've included essential chapters from *The Costa Rica Escape Manual 2019*. Please read or reread them. This is a big decision for you and your family, and you don't want to get blindsided by a water letter. Not sure what that means? You will by the end of this book.

This will be a fun adventure, but there will likely be hiccups along the way. Adventures rarely go as planned, which forces you to live in the moment, go with the flow and explore new ways of living.

You might not find everything you were looking for, but you'll gain something even more valuable—a riveting story to tell.

 Disclaimer

I am not affiliated with any realtor and do not sell real estate or get commissions for any sales. This book is designed to give you a general idea of expenses and help create a budget that suits you best. It is not a substitute for boots-on-the-ground investigation. And why wouldn't you want your boots—or, more accurately, flip-flops—on the ground in Costa Rica? Your day may end on a beach sitting on a piece of driftwood, or watching the sunset while pondering your possibilities. You can't do that from your iPhone in Cincinnati.

Link

Video of the Happier House!

https://youtu.be/5Fd5_m4JZms

The Happier House

Picking A Town

Farmers' Market: Look at those melons!

The Central Valley

"That last page turned is a perfect excuse to write a whole new book."
~Toni Sorenson

In the middle of Costa Rica is an area known as the Central Valley. It's surrounded by mountains and volcanoes and includes the bustling capital of San José. The provinces within the Central Valley are Alajuela, Heredia, San José, and Cartago. There are expat communities throughout, but you'll find a larger number of them in Escazú, Heredia, Grecia, Atenas, and San Ramón.

Living in this area can be beneficial because of its proximity to the San Juan International Airport (also known as the San José airport).

Popular Places: Grecia, Atenas, San Ramón, Escazú

Our first stop when we moved to Costa Rica was **Grecia**, simply because we needed to buy a car. Grecia is known for its many car lots, and there are dozens on either side of the main road. It's where we bought our first car and scooter and ended up living for over three years. It was my first introduction to Costa Rica, and I couldn't imagine it starting any other way.

The Ticos were kind and always made me feel welcome. I saw my first kinkajou and jaguarundi in Grecia, and it's also where I wrote my first book, *Happier Than A Billionaire: Quitting My Job, Moving to Costa Rica, and Living the Zero Hour Work Week.*

Prices were affordable, and we lived on a mountain ridge at an elevation of 4000 feet. Perhaps the lack of oxygen contributed to my happy demeanor. Or maybe it was because I embarked on the best adventure of my life. All I know is that once I stepped foot in this country, my life completely changed. It was as if I could finally catch a breath; I realized I'd been holding mine for over ten years.

San Ramón is a beautiful town north of Grecia. South of Grecia is the popular expat town of **Atenas**. You will want to investigate these areas. Atenas is a little warmer than Grecia, and San Ramón is the rainiest.

Escazú is the priciest since it's near the capital and has everything you can imagine: shopping, restaurants, nightlife, and theaters. It's also a place where many expats must live for work. The embassy and other employers are based here.

You can buy a Big Mac in Escazú and even a MacBook at the nearby San Pedro Apple Store. That's important if you'll need access to the Genius Bar. Most computer repair shops around the country work with Windows operating systems. When my MacBook crashed, I was not a genius, so I waited until I was taking a trip back to New Jersey to drop it off at an Apple Store. I didn't bother driving the four hours to San José, for reasons you'd understand if you have ever driven the four hours to San José.

Naranjo and Sarchi are two other towns to consider in this area. They both have affordable housing and, like Grecia and Atenas, are only an hour from San José.

If you need to be closer to San José but want to be in the countryside, **Cartago** is an excellent spot to check out.

Weather
Dry Season: December to April
Rainy Season: May to November

If there were a beauty pageant for weather, the Central Valley would come in first place for six months of the year. She'd be a gorgeous six-foot model, an accomplished concert pianist, and a Harvard graduate. Temperatures are typically in the seventies in the mountains (21–26°C) and rise to the eighties in the valley (26–32°C). However, there is a significant rainy season here. The roughest time is between September and the end of October. Months of gray, rainy skies make you long for the dry season again.

Because of extreme humidity, you may experience mold in your home. You'd be surprised how much this depends on your elevation. We lived so high on a ridge, clouds blew through our house and covered the walls in condensation, which ultimately led to them covering everything in mold. We had friends who lived a half mile down the road and experienced none of that. Something to think about when house hunting and dream of living in the clouds. Keep in mind, when the dry season comes, you'll be grateful for that same elevation.

Groceries

Most towns in the Central Valley have incredible farmers' markets every week. Hundreds of vendors assemble under a pavilion and sell fruit, eggs, chicken, coffee, and so much more. There are even expats selling their own products. What I liked most about these markets is that their vendors label prices right on the table, so I always knew the cost of everything.

Healthcare

Some of the best private and public hospitals are in this area. If you have a serious medical issue, you may want to live in the Central Valley for its proximity to these facilities. Two private facilities, CIMA Hospital and Hospital Clinica Bíblica, are both Joint Commission International (JCI) accredited. This is a stamp of approval given to health care providers who go through an extensive two-year review.

I've known many expats treated in these hospitals for a variety of illnesses, and their impressions were that it was very similar to care in the United States. But those are private hospitals. Public hospitals can be different, and even though you will get quality care, be prepared for the unexpected. Don't judge a book by its cover, and keep in mind that many doctors will not speak English. For a funny story about Rob getting hernia surgery at one of the least-funded public hospitals, refer to *Happier Than A Billionaire: The Sequel.*

He said, "Stop crying. I'll be okay." (Rob, four days after his hernia surgery at Nicoya Hospital.)

Utilities

Although you will likely not use air conditioning in this cooler climate, you may want to use a dehumidifier if you live in the higher altitudes. Mold can be a problem. Running a dehumidifier all day can easily increase your electric bill by hundreds of dollars.

Guanacaste Province

"The question isn't who is going to let me, it's who is going to stop me."

~Ayn Rand.

Are you looking for a place with white sandy beaches, snorkeling, surfing, and sunset cruises? Guanacaste Province is perfect for those who love lots of sunshine with a mix of Tico culture and tourist excursions.

Many North Americans are attracted to the dry heat, trading in their snow blower in Minneapolis for a boogieboard on Sugar Beach. It was here where I decided that I wanted to move to Costa Rica, and you'll meet many people who felt the same way.

The Liberia Airport (Daniel Oduber Quirós International Airport) is here and adds more flights from around the world every year. Guanacaste is now very accessible, and the increase in tourism has resulted in more infrastructure. I like to brag that there is a paved road from the airport all the way to my house. That's not the biggest deal if you're just visiting, but if you plan on living here, it's a huge amenity. And yes, a paved road is still an amenity in Costa Rica.

Although everyone thinks of beaches when they talk about Guanacaste, the province actually stretches to Arenal Lake, stopping just short of Arenal Volcano. This lake is about two hours from the coast, and the temperatures are much more moderate.

> If you are interested in visiting the Guanacaste area, we would love to host you at The Happier House. For more information on staying with us, send us a message at puravida@happierthanabillionaire.com.

 ### Popular Places: Tamarindo, Potrero, Nosara, Lake Arenal (Tronadora and Nuevo Arenal)

Tamarindo is one of the more touristy towns in Guanacaste. There are tons of activities, restaurants, and an active night-life. If you are young and like to party until three a.m., this is the place for you. If you are older and like to party until three a.m., I have to ask, "How do you have the stamina?" I'm in bed by eight. I put on my pajamas at six. I'm thinking about supper at four.

A good rule of thumb is that everything is less expensive the farther you go from a tourist town. So if you have your heart set on Tamarindo, search a ten-mile radius around the town. The issue here is if you'll have transportation because much of the surrounding area is still made up of sleepy beach towns. But there is usually bus service, even if it isn't as frequent as in more popular areas.

Potrero is still a quiet beach town with both modest and stately homes. It has a lively expat scene, and many restaurants have been opening in the area. There is even a beer distillery and neighboring beer garden. An interesting interview I did with the owner appears in the *The Costa Rica Escape Manual 2019*. It's a wonderful place if you're looking to enjoy the Tamarindo scene, but don't want to live in the middle of all the action.

Nosara is a secluded area in the middle of the Nicoya Peninsula. It's famous for its yoga, incredible surfing, and nearby Ostional Wildlife Reserve. Traveling there will take you over rivers and down dirt roads. There was a time when we had to drive through rivers, but the government has now erected bridges. We're now members of an elite club: The Bridge Prima Donnas. There is a secret handshake.

Near Nosara are the beaches of Pelada and Guiones. They aren't technically in Nosara, which is higher on a hill while these areas are at sea level.

Tronadora, at 2014 feet, has an entirely different climate than at the coast: cooler and wetter. It borders Lake Arenal and has a growing community of expats. If you're a bird photographer, you'll get great shots of thicket antpittas, black-crested coquettes, fasciated tiger-herons, bare-necked umbrellabirds, yellow-eared toucanets, emerald tanagers, and great curassows. You'll also see Woody Woodpecker and Toucan Sam.

Nuevo Arenal is another town that borders the lake and has a lively expat community. I did not pick La Fortuna, the busy tourist town at the base of Arenal Volcano, because it's in Alajuela Province, not Guanacaste. I take pride in my fact checking and will not lead you down the wrong road. But let's just say that everywhere around the lake is pleasant, with cooler and rainier weather.

Playas del Coco and **Sámara** are two other towns to consider in Guanacaste.

Weather

Rainy Season: May to November

Dry Season: December to April

Temperatures are consistently in the mid-eighties to mid-nineties (31–36°C). Guanacaste gets less rain than anywhere else in the country. Tourists can usually enjoy sunny days into the first week of October.

One can find higher elevations, and lower temperatures, near the upper Pacific slopes of the Guanacaste Cordillera and the northern half of the Tilarán Cordillera. These areas are cooler, typically in the seventies and eighties, and support cloud forests.

Healthcare

Since San José is four hours away, you will probably rely on local healthcare facilities such as the public hospitals in Liberia and Nicoya. A private facility, Hospital San Rafael Arcángel, is in Liberia. A doctor there performed my colonoscopy, and I chronicled that experience in my 2016 *Costa Rica Escape Manual*. For three hundred dollars, I was Roto-Rootered by a bilingual doctor who did his internship in Italy. That last detail is of no consequence other than it pleases me to know that Italian ingenuity was involved in diagnosing my irritable bowel syndrome. And not to brag, but he said my colon was "Bellissimo!"—something which I bring up at all dinner parties.

Most towns have clinics available for less urgent situations like stitches, colds, rashes, etc. But for more serious conditions, you will need to get to Nicoya or Liberia. And for the most serious, you might eventually end up in San José.

Utilities

Because of the heat, many people use air conditioning, and your electric bill will reflect that. You may also have a large water bill if you plan on irrigating your landscaping. For that reason, many people choose drought-tolerant plants.

The moment I saw scarlet macaws fly overhead. Nothing in my life would ever be the same.

Southern Pacific Coast

"A diamond is merely a lump of coal that did well under pressure."

~Unknown

I've got the perfect road trip for you. Hop onto Route 34 (the Costanera Highway) and meander down the Pacific coast toward Jacó, Manuel Antonio, Dominical and Uvita. The roadside fast food is a guy selling pipa frias (cold coconuts). Your parking lot is a sandy patch under a palm tree.

I love taking this trip and often get lost in dreamy thoughts. We drove this route soon after we moved to Costa Rica. I have a picture of myself on the beach with a big smile on my face. I had just seen a scarlet macaw fly overhead. My life forever changed at that moment, and yours likely will too.

Popular Places: Jacó, San Isidro de El General, Dominical and Quepos

Jacó is one of the more popular tourist towns in Costa Rica. With its proximity to the capital (only an hour and a half away), it's a common vacation destination for people flying into the San Juan Airport (San José airport). It has a prominent nightlife, and every time I've heard of someone having a bachelor party in Costa Rica, it's always in Jacó.

San Isidro de El General is two hours southeast from Jacó. It's not a beach town but is located at 2200 meters above sea level. This affords you cooler weather all year round. San Isidro has a lot to offer: restaurants, medical facilities, and shopping. It also has a large farmers' market, similar to what you would find near San José. It reminds me very much of Grecia.

Quepos is a harbor town popular for sport fishing. It has a lively expat community and is near the famous Manuel Antonio National Park. If you are looking to live around monkeys, this is the place.

Dominical is the quintessential surfing town. It's also close to Nauyaca Waterfalls. At three stories, it's everything a waterfall should be. Once you visit this town, and all of its happy surfers, you may never look at your life the same way again.

Although I don't cover them here, **Uvita and Ojochal** are other beach towns you may want to investigate. They are both popular places for expats.

Weather

Dry Season: Mid- December to April

Rainy Season: April to Mid-December

Temperatures are usually in the high eighties (26–32°Celsius), and it can cool off into the low seventies at night (21–23°Celsius). This area has a substantial rainy season, with September and October being the wettest. The humidity is often higher when compared to Guanacaste.

Healthcare

If you live in Jacó, it's not too far of a drive to medical facilities in San José. If that's too far, all the towns listed have private clinics that perform many small procedures and emergency services.

In Quepos, Dominical, and Uvita, you'll rely on the hospital in San Isidro for larger medical issues (an hour and a half from Quepos, forty-five minutes from Dominical, and an hour and twenty minutes from Uvita).

Utilities

Because of the heat, air conditioning will be your biggest expense, and your electric bill will reflect that.

Caribbean

"A laugh is a smile that bursts."
~ Mary H. Waldrip

Roll down your window and follow the reggae music. The Caribbean is one of the most beautiful places in Costa Rica. Although less developed, it's hard not to fall in love with the area. There's something about turquoise water that makes you dream of all the things worth dreaming about.

The Port of Limón is located on the Caribbean coast and is where many goods arrive in the country. Travel south along Route 36 and meander down the shoreline. The salty air power washes your worries, scrubs away the patina, and uncovers a shinier, happier person. If you are a sloth lover, I've seen more here than anywhere else in the country.

Be advised that you will be quite a distance away from the San José airport (a four-and-a-half-hour drive on a good day). There is a small landing strip south of Limón where you can board a Cessna from Sansa Airlines.

The Places: Cahuita, Puerto Viejo, Playa Chiquita

Cahuita is forty-five minutes south of Limón and is home to Cahuita National Park. There are two beautiful beaches located here: Playa Blanca and Puerto Vargas.

Puerto Viejo is fifteen minutes south of Cahuita and is a major hub for backpackers. This is one of their last stops before heading to Panama. It's a fun town with restaurants, accommodations, and shopping. But be aware you will not find a Four Seasons here, or a Westin— so if that's your standard of travel, you'll want to look elsewhere.

Playa Chiquita is 3.7 miles south of Puerto Viejo and doesn't have much of a town center. But it does have a quiet beach and some reasonable rental options.

Weather

The Caribbean side of Costa Rica is one of the wettest parts of the country and has a wacky weather pattern. The rainiest months are usually June and November. Summer months are typically September and October. In other words, count on a lot of rain most of the year. Temperatures remain relatively consistent, in the low nineties (32-34°C) during the day and high seventies (25-26°C) at night.

Healthcare

The nearest hospital is in Limón. There's a small medical office in Puerto Viejo that can treat small issues.

If you are dealing with medical issues, be aware that this is a less developed area of the country. Even though Costa Rica looks small on a map, it takes a while to get anywhere. Many times there's just one road going through an area, and when that closes, you can be stuck in traffic for hours.

Utilities

This area is more humid than in any other place in Costa Rica. You may want to use air conditioning for most of the day. There may also be intermittent interruptions to the water and electric supply.

Finding a Home

Tico-Style Home

Housing Styles

"It's always too early to quit."
~ Norman Vincent Peale

To help you understand homes in Costa Rica, I broke them down into three different styles: Tico style, moderately appointed, and gringo style. I've lived in all three throughout my years here. Whether you'll be renting or buying, this information pertains to you.

Tico Style

When house hunting in Costa Rica, you may notice that some homes are advertised as "Tico style." These are usually smaller homes that may not have all the modern conveniences you might be used to. A Tico home could have low ceilings, the inability to flush toilet paper, oddly proportioned furniture, or a suicide shower. There will be no fancy granite countertops or high-end appliances. There might not even be kitchen cabinets. It's a very basic home that includes just the bare necessities.

What a Tico house is likely to have is beautiful landscaping, and possibly a spectacular view. You can't ask for more after drinking a cup of coffee while watching magpies break open your papayas and coatis waddling through your yard. I've lived in homes that were only a short walk away from some of the most beautiful waterfalls and in communities with the best neighbors.

When touring these homes, keep an open mind. Happiness is not always found in square footage or fancy furnishings.

Moderately Appointed

These homes rent for a few hundred dollars more than a Tico-style house. They'll have a proper septic system and hot water throughout. They could even have a washer and dryer. If you've read my previous books, you know I use the phrase "results may vary." And results will vary when renting or buying these homes.

I've lived in this category as well and found not everything was in working order. The outlets weren't grounded, or there were on-demand hot water units that didn't provide enough hot water. But that never bothered us enough to move. I was just happy to be out of my office and off on a new adventure. My accommodations were an afterthought.

This can be a rental sweet spot. You will have much more wiggle room and may find something that feels more like home. You're out of the "suicide shower" category, and you'll be able to flush your toilet paper without a care in the world. Pop the champagne bottle and make a toast. I believe in celebrating every milestone.

Gringo Style

If you can't live without a bathtub, granite countertops, GE appliances, and more than one bedroom, this is the category for you. These are higher-end homes; I have never seen a suicide shower in this price range. The building style is similar to homes in the United States or Canada. All this comes with a higher price tag, and you'll be surprised how much you can live without if you choose one of the other two categories.

 Ramblings

In some listings, I mention when a property does not have air conditioning. This may or may not be a concern for you, but parts of the country can get hot during certain times of the year. Ticos are used to the heat, but not all gringos find it comfortable.

There are also many parts of Costa Rica at higher elevations, such as the Central Valley, where the weather is cooler and there is simply no need for air conditioning.

Regardless of the category, there is always a chance there will be bars on the windows. This is not always an indication of a crime problem. In Tico culture, they can actually be a status symbol. Many people find them attractive, and it says to neighbors that they have something worth protecting.

Costa Rica is a country of personal responsibility. They do not rely heavily on the police or fire department. They are more likely to take extra measures to protect their property. Please read *The Costa Rica Escape Manual 2019* to learn more about crime in Costa Rica.

Different Strokes

"I always wanted to be somebody, but now I realize I should have been more specific."
~Lily Tomlin

Before we pick a town, there are things you need to understand before beginning your housing search. Standards are different in Costa Rica, especially in older homes. Some things may feel a tad weird, like when you see electrical wires coming out of a shower wall. The owner of the house may be standing alongside you when you notice this, so don't be rude and yell, "Oh no. I could never live here!" Instead say, "How about that!" You'll look like a swell guy, and people will enjoy having you around.

> A cordial disposition gets you farther than yelling in this country. Once you blow up, it's hard to put that genie back in the bottle.

Electric

Electricity is very expensive, and stores will often shut off their overhead lights. When I first came to Costa Rica, I thought shops were closed because of their darkened interiors. After paying your first electric bill, you'll understand this completely.

You may encounter houses where the electricity is not grounded properly. Nearly every expat has lost an appliance to electrical surges. When house hunting, **bring along an outlet tester**.

Whether or not the outlets are grounded, it's always good to pack many high-quality surge protectors. I even have one on my washing machine. I witnessed a motherboard explode when I lived in the mountains. The part alone cost $175 from a local shop in town.

The Toilet Paper Caper

It's not that uncommon to find a house, or restaurant, that has a septic system that cannot handle toilet paper. It gets disposed not in the bowl but in a trash can alongside the commode. Let's look on the bright side: the majority of what's important still gets flushed.

At first, this seems weird, but it's best to just get past it and not be like the gringos who loudly complain that it's unacceptable. Do you know what's unacceptable? Someone yelling about toilet paper after walking out of a restaurant bathroom while you're still eating. Just stay calm and move on. Or better yet, say, "How about that!" and go back to enjoying your gallo pinto.

Suicide Showers

You may also find an affordable rental that has a strange donut-shaped ceramic device as a showerhead. That is affectionately called a suicide shower. It's as fun as it sounds! Some houses aren't plumbed for hot water, so an electrical heating element is wired into the shower head. Yes... you read that right. It's wired right into the shower you'll be standing in. I like to call this high-stakes bathing. And whatever you do, don't touch it while the shower is running, as my girlfriend did. She survived the shock but was a little squirrely for a few days. This is another "How about that!" moment.

Suicide Shower

Hard Hot Water Throughout... But not in the Bathtub

You little trust fund baby. Now you're living the life with a rental that has hot water coming out of your shower, a kitchen sink and a washing machine. It makes a big difference because Costa Rica has hard water, and without hot water, it's challenging to get dishes and clothing clean.

More expensive homes may have a water softener, but I never rented one that did. We don't have a water softener in our house because our septic tank recycles the water. After going through a cleaning process, the gray water is spat out and irrigates our bougainvillea plants (the salt in a water softener could damage them). I don't mean to brag, but you've never seen such gorgeous bougainvillea bushes as the ones at The Happier House. And all my guests have contributed to their loveliness. Some more than others.

When investigating rentals, look to see where their hot water originates. From a hot water heater? If so, you'll have a higher electric bill. In one rental, we shut off the hot water heater until we knew we were taking a shower. Rob and I coordinated our showering just to save money. It's as romantic as it sounds.

You may notice metal boxes under sinks in the bathroom and kitchen. These are on-demand hot water heaters, or as I like to call them, "Don't-demand-too-much-hot-water heaters." They heat the water just fine, as long as you keep your faucet at a trickle. As a result, you end up sitting in just a half inch of hot water, which makes you feel stupid.

If the house has a solar water heater, this is great. We have a large one, and it helps lower our electric bill. And it's nice to fill up our tub with water heated by the sun. I call it sunshine water.

Appliances

I suspect that appliances are of lower quality here. My only proof of this is that they often need repairing. It drives everyone nuts, so don't be surprised if your expat friend asks you to haul down a Vitamix, which is something we recently did because our blenders quickly blend themselves into oblivion.

One time we purchased a coffeemaker and asked if it had a warranty. "Yes, one year," the clerk said. But the company was Durabrand, and if you've ever owned anything of theirs, you realize there is nothing durable about it. When Rob inquired again, the clerk took out a binder and looked up the model and said, "Yes, it's a thirty-day warranty."

So we enjoyed lukewarm coffee for a whopping forty-five days before it conked out (see *Repairs*).

Repairs

We then took it to a repairman who replaced the heating element for ten dollars. It worked for another ten months before it was laid to rest in our appliance graveyard.

Everything gets repaired here; it's not a throwaway society because of high import taxes. Labor is reasonable, but parts are very expensive.

How do you fix the internet? Stick a soda bottle on top.

Alcatraz

Another thing that shocks people is that many houses have bars on their windows or walls around their house. Costa Rica does not have a police force similar to those in the United States. There are not enough tax dollars. Petty theft is a problem here, and if someone burglarizes your house, the police may or may not show up. To mitigate the chances of this happening, personal responsibility is advised. This could mean bars on your windows, security cameras, etc.

If you've read my other books, you already know that my husband takes this seriously. Super seriously. You can take a guy out of Brooklyn—that's it, you can take a guy out of Brooklyn. Read my first book if you want to know a secret place to hide a weapon. Spoiler alert: have a fire extinguisher handy. Or, pick up the *The Costa Rica Escape Manual 2019*, where you can read about some of the ridiculous methods my husband has used to scare off criminals.

I lived in houses with bars. After a while, you don't even notice them. It's as if your brain tricks you into seeing right past them. And just because you see bars doesn't mean you are in a bad community. It's just how things are done here and can be considered a status symbol. They mean you have something to lose.

Size Matters

In many cases, the square footage of a house includes outdoor space. So if a listing reads 1200 feet, it may comprise a tiny house with a glorious patio out back. I've seen homes listed as 5000 square feet, only to find most of it was a giant carport.

A rental listed as a casita is usually someone's guesthouse or a small residence. Either way, it will not be a sprawling estate. But it certainly doesn't mean it isn't attractive. I'll take a 400 square foot casita surrounded by fruit trees over a 5000 square foot mansion surrounded by a cement wall.

Neighbors

Zoning laws are random throughout the country. You may find that the perfect rental is right next door to a rooster academy. You may even discover that your neighbor is a mechanic and paints cars, all day, every day, and ten feet from your kitchen window. Visit the house at various times of the day to find out what you may be dealing with.

Laundry

For reasons unbeknownst to me, there are few laundromats in Costa Rica. This is a concern if you're renting a house without a washing machine. There are also few dry cleaners, so leave those ball gowns at home.

And for all you cocky Tide users, that detergent is expensive here. You may have to kiss those whitey-whites goodbye for a while if you plan to live on a strict budget.

Closets

I've been in million-dollar homes with closets that are just shelves on a wall. Others don't have closets at all. It could be because you don't need any winter clothes here, so a walk-in closet is a rare find.

Garages

Many homes, even the pricier ones, may lack a garage. Some only have carports. This is important if you're a handy guy who has tools you plan to ship down. Where are you going to store them? Consider that before committing to taking them with you.

 **Ramblings**

The best part about moving to another country is that everything is different. But there will be times when things feel a little too different. In less expensive rentals, you may find that the ceilings are low, the couches are uncomfortable, the tile choices are unattractive, and there are weird fixtures throughout. This can surprise North Americans who haven't lived in these types of homes before.

A strange feeling bubbles up, like a homesickness burp. These homes can feel so foreign you'll want to head back toward the airport until you notice a troop of monkeys dangling from a guanacaste tree. Pause and watch them. Take a deep breath. Sad feelings don't have to fill all the room in your head. Allow the happy ones to rise to the surface.

When you feel the beginning of a homesickness burp, just remember that this rental may not be your forever place. Give yourself time to adapt and keep an open mind.

Searching for Listings

"If you don't know where you are going, you might wind up someplace else."

~Yogi Berra

There are four ways you should go about searching for rentals or real estate:

Facebook

Facebook is an excellent source to find housing. Once you decide which place to live, search Facebook groups that end in "chit chat," "classified ads," or "garage sale." Some great groups are:

- Atenas Costa Rica Classifieds
- Tamarindo Chit Chat
- Potrero Garage Sale
- Nosara Classified Ads
- Lake Arenal Garage Sale/Fortuna Garage Sale
- Manuel Antonio/Quepos Garage Sale
- Dominical & Uvita: Ride Share/Carpool-Trades/Services/Items 4 Sale/Rentals
- Puerto Viejo Buy and Sell

There are many general Facebook expat groups where you can ask questions, but that may or may not give you the specific information you need. I would narrow down where you want to live first and head straight to groups specifically for that town.

Realtors

Realtors are always a great source for listings. A reputable one knows the community and is the first to hear when a good deal opens up. When visiting Costa Rica, stop by a few and see if they have any leads.

Be advised, just because a realtor has a big corporate name attached to it doesn't make it any more reputable.

Craigslist

Craigslist.org does not have as many listings as it had before Facebook came along. So many people are gravitating towards social media to list their places that Craigslist is almost an afterthought. But I wouldn't exclude them either. Use every resource available to you—and I found some interesting places listed there that weren't on Facebook.

Word of Mouth

Word of mouth is still the better way to find the best bargain. Don't worry if you have to settle for a less-than-ideal rental when you first move here. You will eventually find your perfect spot after making friends.

Rents exceeding $1145 are now subject to a 13% VAT. When searching for listings, ask if the tax is included in the price.

In the middle of construction of The Happier House. Our dream was finally coming true.

When to Rent: The Christmas & Easter Conundrum

"We never really grow up, we only learn how to act in public."

~Bryan White

Mildred just found a real estate listing in a Facebook group that looks perfect.

"Doug, this is the place!" she hollers across the living room to her husband. "It's only two blocks from the beach, it has three bedrooms and air conditioning, and we can even flush our toilet paper! The rent is only seven hundred dollars a month!"

Mildred and Doug make an appointment to see the listing and are immediately impressed. They're ready to sign the lease, but they notice a paragraph stating the tenants must vacate the premises, with all of their belongings, for two weeks during Christmas and another two weeks around Easter.

"I don't understand. We're supposed to move out of the house and return after two weeks?"

"Yep," the landlord says.

Welcome to house hunting in Costa Rica.

The Christmas and Easter holidays are the busiest times for vacation rentals in Costa Rica. If you live near a tourist town, your rent may reflect that increased demand. Even if it's a long-term lease, the landlord may stipulate before the signing that he wants you out so he can rent during those holiday weeks for a higher profit as a vacation rental. Rob and I had to leave our rentals many times, and I can tell you, it gets old fast. We were on such a strict budget, we didn't have much of a choice. But perhaps you do.

"What if we didn't want to leave during the holidays?" Doug asks the landlord. "Can't we sign a normal one-year lease?"

Of course you can, Doug, and thanks for speaking up. It's always good to negotiate and not throw in the towel once you hit an obstacle. That's rule number one in Costa Rica: Never let a roadblock stop you from enjoying the view. Unless it's at a cliff. Keep your distance in that case.

At this point, Mildred is hopeful. She has already fallen in love with the house, and it's even fenced in for when she adopts a dog from the nearby animal rescue. And let's be honest, Mildred is tired. This move to Costa Rica was exhausting, and she's eager to start this next phase of her life. This is about the time the landlord chimes in, "You can rent it without leaving for the holidays, for eighteen hundred dollars a month."

"But that's more than double the rate!" Doug yells.

Yes. Yes, it is, Doug.

I don't want to be a Debbie Downer since this won't always be the case. If you choose a town that isn't a tourist hub, you'll likely never encounter this situation. But even when we lived in Grecia, we had landlords asking us to leave when they decided to return for their yearly vacation. Or we lived in homes that were on the market, so we had people coming through every few days. We had many years of feeling displaced, which is why I'm so thankful for The Happier House today.

Another important consideration is the timing of your move. If you're relocating to a touristy town in December and need a long-term rental, you'll likely have a hard time finding anything reasonable.

> If possible, plan your move for after the New Year. And never search for rentals right before Easter.

So where did this leave Doug and Mildred? Mildred walked into the backyard and sulked, but Doug didn't give up. He negotiated the landlord down to fifteen hundred dollars a month and crossed out the paragraph regarding leaving for the holidays. They did find their happy place. It cost more than they expected, but now that they have boots on the ground, they'll have a better chance of finding something cheaper when their lease ends.

The good news is that when you finally find your place and settle in, you can unwind. This is all one grand adventure, and it's the reason you became an expat. When you hang up your clothes, stock your pantry, and look out at all the parrots in your yard, you'll realize how far you've come. And that's something worth celebrating.

Buying Land & Squatters' Rights

"Wisdom comes from experience. Experience is often a result of lack of wisdom."
  ~ Terry Pratchett

Believe it or not, squatters (people who show up on your property and pitch a tent, build a house, or just sit in a lawn chair) can obtain rights to your property. "This is ridiculous! How can this happen?" you ask. Take a deep breath, because I don't have a satisfying explanation for you.

Many people come to Costa Rica and buy a large parcel, hoping to one day build a house or start a development. They return home and put the idea on the back burner, assuming all is well since they own the deed to the land. "In ten years we'll build our dream home there," Chuck says to his wife. Then that day comes, and the back burner is blazing up the place. Lo and behold, a family is living on the property, and things have become complicated.

Squatters (or *precaristas* as they're called in Costa Rica) can acquire rights to a property if it's left abandoned or unmaintained. Of course it's abandoned and unmaintained because you're living outside the country and going about your business. Who thinks about visiting a property just to make sure someone didn't pitch a tent on it?

Squatters are attracted to rural areas or unfenced lots. They can set up a homestead, start a farm, or even fence in your property. They may even do so while taking selfies. These act as proof they can present to the courts. If they can convince authorities that the land has been "improved," they will have squatters' rights. How long do they have to do this to establish these rights?

More than twelve months.

Yes. You read that right. In just over one year, according to Article 279 of the Costa Rican civil code, a person can gain rights to property by means of occupation. Once these rights are established, you cannot evict them. The only recourse is to file a lawsuit.

Legal Recourse

Squatting Less than Three Months

It's imperative to catch squatters as quickly as possible. If they've been on your land for less than three months, you can call the police. You should be ready with as much information as possible: papers identifying you as the true owner, witnesses that have seen them illegally encroach on your land, and photographs of the invasion. The police should evict them at this point, but they may not. Just because you are in the right does not mean things will always go your way.

Squatting More than Three Months but Less than a Year

The owner must file a trespassing complaint (*usurpación*). At this point, the eviction process starts, and it could be some time before the police evict them from the premises. The trespassers may request money for the improvements they made to your property.

Squatting Over a Year

Hire a good lawyer, because you're in for a lengthy fight in the court system.

How to Avoid It

1. Buy a property in a gated community or from a developer that can help watch over the land.
2. Hire a legal caretaker—this is further proof you own the land and are actively caring for it.
3. Build fences around the property. Take pictures of all the work and improvements you are doing.
4. Always pay your taxes on time. This is further proof you haven't abandoned the property.

Although it sounds crazy, you can avoid getting caught up in this if you do a little homework. Is a realtor showing you land with people living on it? Investigate that further and find out if these people have already established squatters' rights. Are you buying a large piece of land and disappearing for a while? Hire a management company to care for it, and demand a contract. Ask for pictures throughout the year to ensure they're maintaining the property.

Ramblings

Now you may wonder, "Nadine, have you seen this happen in person?" And sadly, the answer is yes.

There was a rumor that a neighbor in Grecia had passed away. Someone came and mowed the lawn for over a year. It turns out the neighbor was in the hospital but got better. He returned to Costa Rica and found a squatter had already obtained rights to his land. I don't know how all this ended, but I suppose the moral to this story is to make sure you eat your vegetables, exercise regularly, and don't end up in the hospital.

If I do drop dead, kindly use my body as a scarecrow. String me up between the papaya and the banana plants (preferably in reach of Rob's sprinklers), and point me toward the ocean view. This is a wonderful way to spend all of eternity.

Another side effect of not maintaining a piece of land is that endangered trees may grow where you may later intend to build your home. Cutting them down can lead to hefty fines and incarceration. See the 2019 *Escape Manual* for more information on this subject.

Real Estate & The Maritime Zone

"The need for change bulldozed a road down the center of my mind."
~ Maya Angelou

Are you interested in beachfront property? Found a house that is only a few steps from the water's edge? If so, you'll want to dive headfirst into this chapter. There are crucial title differences between beachfront versus inland property.

What is the Maritime Zone?

Costa Rica designates the Maritime Zone as the first 200 meters from the water's edge at high tide.

The first 50 meters from high tide is considered the public area, where there is no allowance for any building. This zone includes rocks, estuaries, mangroves, and any natural formation. Since there are no private beaches in Costa Rica, this area is open to everyone. The Ticos are proud of this. They can never understand how other countries make people pay for access to beaches. "It all belongs to God," said one local, and I agree.

Within the remaining 150 meters you cannot own anything, but you can build a structure with approval from government agencies for an annual fee. This annual fee is called a concession (*concesiones*) and is extended to you by the municipality. If granted, follow their zoning laws and comply with their regulatory plan (*plan regulador*). You will not have a title as you would if you had bought a property further inland.

How long is a concession valid?

Concessions are leased for periods of fifteen years and up. They automatically renew as long as you're in good standing and have built nothing that conflicts with the regulatory plan. The National Registry should have the property already on file. If it isn't, there's no reason to investigate any further. Walk away and be happy you didn't get caught up in a costly mistake

Who can get a concession?

- Residents with a minimum of five years living in Costa Rica
- Costa Rican nationals
- Costa Rican corporations with at least 50% Costa Rican ownership

- People who have obtained a "Tourist Declaration" from the government (you need a good lawyer for this)

Can the government take away a concession?

Yes, they can. It will involve a lengthy court fight, with them trying to prove you broke the conditions of the law.

Ramblings

I pass beautiful homes along the beach every day. They have balconies welcoming soirees of salty breezes into their bedrooms. Everything looks perfect until everything isn't. Do your homework with these properties and make sure all the t's are crossed and i's are dotted. Your contract has to be as solid as a rock to avoid litigation in the future.

"Nadine, are you aware of the government seizing any properties?" you ask. Unfortunately, I am. One was my favorite hotel on the Caribbean side. The owners fought a lengthy court battle and lost. Then one day bulldozers showed up and leveled the entire structure. I don't know the details of the case, or who was in the right or in the wrong. It's a good example of how you never know with whom the courts will side. An experienced real estate agent and attorney and your own due diligence can help you avoid this catastrophe.

"We'll grow our own food!" Rob said. "It'll only cost a few hundred dollars in PVC and plastic."

Then a gust of wind spectacularly blew our Grecia greenhouse off the mountain.

Fortunately, I was not in it at the time.

House Hunting: Central Valley

"I'm here today because I refused to be unhappy. I took a chance. "
~Wanda Sykes

The following are average costs of renting or purchasing a home in Grecia, Atenas, San Ramón, and Escazú. A small description follows each listing and may help you decide if that price range is something you can live with. Due to copyright issues, I could not include pictures of each home, but after a quick search on the internet, you will find something similar (see the chapter "Searching for Listings").

To use this chapter:
1. Decide whether you are renting or buying.
2. Pick one of the four towns.
3. Choose which category matches your budget.

Renting on a $1200 per Month Budget:
Tico Style

Grecia

$400/month | Partially Furnished | 3 bed, 1 bath | 1100 sq. feet
This home is on the lovely mountain ridge of San Isidro de Grecia. This means you'll have temperatures in the seventies most of the year! But this lower rent has some caveats. Namely, there is a suicide shower. When rents are this low, you may also not be able to flush your toilet paper. But look on the bright side: it includes three beds, a sofa, stove, refrigerator, and washing machine! And you're near a bus stop, so you won't need to buy a car.

Atenas

$395/month | Furnished | 1 bed, 1 bath | 750 sq. feet
A comfortable casita on 2.5 acres and surrounded by fruit trees.

San Ramón

$400/month | Unfurnished | 2 beds, 1 bath | 850 sq. feet
A small home, near a bus stop and close to neighbors. It has a nice-sized backyard with fruit trees.

Escazú

In this price range, you will most likely be looking for a condominium, and it'll be located outside of Escazú. Some include swimming pools, a gym, conference rooms, video room, game rooms, underground parking, laundry facilities, and rooftop clubhouses. These run around $450/month and up. Quality varies at this price range, but you can find a good deal if you give yourself time to search through many listings.

 ## Renting on a $2500 per Month Budget: Moderately Appointed

Grecia
$700/month | Furnished | 2 beds, 1 bath | 1450 sq. feet
Located high on a mountaintop overlooking a coffee farm, this home includes a washer and dryer. I've lived on a coffee farm, and it was ironic being surrounded by caffeine at a point when I was the calmest I've ever been in my entire life. You're near a bus stop but about a twenty-minute drive from town.

Atenas
$800/month | Furnished | 2 beds, 1 bath | 750 sq. feet
This casita has a distant ocean view and a shared pool. Yes, it is possible to see the ocean from Atenas on a clear day. There's a garden full of fruit trees, and if that's not awesome enough, this price includes utilities.

San Ramón
$700/month | Furnished | 1 bed, 1 bath | 800 sq. feet
A secluded home, surrounded by lush gardens, and six miles from the center of town. It's perfect for a person who dreams of writing a novel. Getting rid of distractions in your life is the best way to bring out your inner creativity.

Escazú

$750/month | Furnished | 2 beds, 1 bath | 750 sq. feet
An apartment near the Multiplaza (a big mall in Escazú). It has a washer and dryer. You'll be near public transportation, and it's perfect for someone who isn't purchasing a vehicle but still needs to get their MacBook fixed.

Renting on a $3500 per Month budget: Gringo Style

Homes will likely now resemble what you are used to. I have never seen a suicide shower in this price range, but I wouldn't count that luxury item out. You never know what you'll find while house hunting in Costa Rica.

Grecia

$1000/month | Furnished | 3 beds, 2 baths | 1300 sq. feet
A new private home up on the San Isidro mountain ridge. The house is on a family farm and has an abundance of fruit trees. You'll have bananas, guys. Lots and lots of bananas.

Atenas

$1500/month | Furnished | 3 beds, 3 1/2 baths | 2000 sq. feet
Airy tropical home with mountain views from the second story and a guest bedroom with its own bathroom. You'll never have to share one when your husband's weird friend from high school visits. It comes with a fully equipped kitchen with custom cabinets, laundry room, dining room, and a bedroom with access to a terrace. It's completely fenced in with an electric gate, alarm system, and security cameras.

San Ramón

$1500/month | Furnished | 4 beds, 3 baths | 2100 sq. feet
This home includes a carport, security cameras, and a nice-sized backyard. Since it's a little far from town, you will need a car with this listing.

Escazú

$1250/month | Unfurnished | 3 beds, 2 1/2 baths | 1900 sq. feet
Near a bus stop with all the comforts you're used to. Granite countertops and a backyard. Includes 24-hour security.

• •

 ## Purchasing Real Estate: Under $150,000

Grecia

$115,000 | 2 beds, 1 bath | 1100 sq. feet | .25 acres
At 4000 feet, this area of Grecia is very popular for its views and cooler climate. The yard is fully fenced, and there's a gate and alarm system installed. Only fifteen minutes from Grecia, but with no bus route, so you'll need a car. The kitchen features granite countertops and a large dining area.

Atenas

$125,000 | 2 beds, 1 bath | 1130 sq. feet | .09 acre
A simple home with walking distance to the center of town. This is perfect for someone who's downsizing and wants low maintenance.

San Ramón

$85,000 | 3 beds, 2 baths | 1 acre

A Tico-style home located twenty-five minutes from the center of town. It's advertised as a "private, silent house." I would ruin everything since I can't shut up for more than ten minutes. On the other hand, my husband would love this place.

Escazú

$130,000 | 3 beds, 2 baths | 2010 sq. feet

A two-story townhouse with parking for two cars and access to a community pool and clubhouse.

 ## Purchasing Real Estate: $150,000–$250,000

Grecia

$159,000 | 3 beds, 2 baths | 1900 sq. feet | .25 acres

Ten minutes by car from the center of town, with lots of trees and mature landscaping. There are beautiful hardwood finishings throughout the house. It's in a quiet area yet close to public transportation. Listing includes high-end stainless steel appliances.

Atenas

$265,000 | 2 beds, 2 baths | 2196 sq. feet | .3 acres

This brand-new home has a great view and ample privacy. It features fifteen feet cathedral ceilings, granite countertops, and an infinity pool. There's a guest house with a private outdoor deck, plus an alarm system, security cameras, and an in-ground irrigation system.

San Ramón

$175,000 | 3 beds, 2 baths | 1500 sq. feet | .2 acres
Distant views of the Gulf of Nicoya and the Pacific Ocean. Includes a large patio, carport, and a chicken coop. It's a five-minute walk to a bus stop ten-minute drive to the center of town.

Escazú

$199,000 | 2 beds, 2 baths | 1937 sq. feet | .14 acres
This home is located just blocks from downtown Escazú and features a treehouse, shed, an outdoor pizza oven, and enough parking for four cars. It also includes a guest apartment.

 ## Purchasing Real Estate: $250,000–$375,000

Grecia

$300,000 | 2 beds, 2.5 baths | 2400 sq. feet | .25 acres
This home is close to town yet still secluded, and you can enjoy your seclusion while picking bananas from your fruit trees. There's is even mood lighting and a large terrace.

Atenas

$375,000 | 3 beds, 2 baths | 1938 sq. feet | 10.6 acres
This jungle home is perfect for the person who's more interested in land than all the amenities a new home offers. It features hot water throughout, two stalls for horses, and a two-car garage. Although modest, this listing comes with breathtaking acreage that's hard to pass up.

San Ramón

$265,000 | 1 bed, 1.5 bath + guesthouse | 1500 sq. feet | .33 acres
The property is within walking distance to stores and has a bus stop nearby. It's all one level and features vaulted ceilings, granite countertops, a walk-in closet and access to a separate studio apartment. The master bath has a bathtub and a solar water heater to fill it. There's a one- bedroom, one-bathroom guest house for all those friends that will come to visit you.

Escazú

$350,000 | 3 beds, 2 1/2 baths | 4050 sq. feet | .10 acre
A two-story home in a gated community, only five minutes to downtown Escazú. Home features a carport, granite countertops, large closets, and access to the shared pool and gazebo. It's also a whopping 4050 sq. feet!

 ## Purchasing Real Estate: $375,000–$500,000

Grecia

$380,000 | 3 beds, 2 baths | 3800 sq. feet | .25 acres
This two-story home features a large kitchen, dining area, Jacuzzi tub, walk-in closet, covered terrace, and gorgeous views of the mountains. It's in a gated community with amenities such as a pool, rancho, and 24-hour security.

Atenas

$364,000 | 3 beds, 2.5 baths | 3229 sq. feet | .24 acres
A furnished home in a gated community and within walking distance to town. This listing features two carports, almond wood ceilings, a covered patio, incredible views, fruit trees, an

irrigation system, and a solar-heated pool. The alarm system includes an exterior laser beam across the property.

San Ramón

$457,000 | 3 beds, 2 baths | 50 acres

In a rural setting thirty-five minutes outside of San Ramón, this home has two corrals and a staging area for cattle. I don't know about you, but I'm always looking for a place to show my livestock. The home features almond ceilings, mountain views, and a wraparound deck. It also comes with a caretaker's home, a vehicle, and an ATV.

Escazú

$499,000 | 3 beds, 3 baths | 3600 sq. feet

A fourth-floor condominium with great views of the countryside. The community offers 24-hour security and a gym.

 ## Purchasing Real Estate: Over $500,000

Grecia

$700,000 | 6 beds, 6 baths | 11,000 sq. feet | 9 acres

Perfect for nature lovers, this home is surrounded by wildlife and has views of the Central Valley, as well as coffee and sugarcane fields. It might be suitable for a bed and breakfast. There's solar hot water and a river at the bottom of the property near a small cabin. This listing also includes a pool, rancho, barbecue area, a bar, full kitchen, bathrooms, and changing areas.

Atenas

$650,000 | 3 beds, 3.5 baths | 4443 sq. feet | 1.7 acres

An elegantly appointed home with all the comforts one could imagine, including a guest house for when family comes to visit. There's an open floor plan, expansive glass sliding doors, a pool, lush gardens, vaulted wood ceilings, and a dream kitchen. For outdoor entertaining, there's also a rancho with a barbecue.

San Ramón

$800,000 | 5 beds, 5 baths | 8987 sq. feet | 1.02 acres

This listing is a spacious two-story home with beautiful mountain views. Home features Jacuzzi tubs, a wrought-iron spiral staircase, granite countertops, a professionally landscaped backyard, and a pool. If you have a large family and desire a lot of living space, this could be the right home for you.

Escazú

$725,000 | 3 beds, 2 baths | 5100 sq. feet | .5 acres

This is a mini estate on Embassy Row. It's a five-minute drive to CIMA hospital and within walking distance of the Multiplaza Mall. Fenced in and beautifully landscaped, with a two-car garage, a driving circle, fireplace, yoga room, travertine floors, and a covered terrace, this listing is nicely appointed. There is a babbling creek and the master bedroom has high ceilings, recessed lighting, a balcony, and check this out—a twenty-two foot bathroom countertop with enough "space for your perfumes."

Who's the lady with that much perfume? I got rid of mine because Rob said it gave him a headache. I get a headache just imagining the smell of this woman.

Ramblings

I've never comfortably swum in any pool in the Central Valley without suffering hypothermia. Especially if the pool is located high on a mountain ridge. My husband can, but I'm a wimp. If you're like me, don't let a pool be the deciding factor when choosing the right house for you. We'll save that one for if you plan on moving to the beach.

The Happier House

House Hunting: Guanacaste

"You'll never find rainbows if you're looking down."
~Charlie Chaplin

The following are average costs of renting or purchasing a home in Tamarindo, Potrero, Nosara, Tronadora, Nuevo Arenal. A small description follows each listing and may help you decide if that price range is something you can live with. Due to copyright issues, I could not include pictures of each home, but after a quick search on the internet, you will find something similar (see chapter "Searching for Listings").

To use this chapter:
1. Decide whether you're renting or buying.
2. Pick one of the five towns.
3. Choose which category matches your budget.

Renting on a $1200 per Month Budget: Tico Style

Tamarindo
$275/month | Shared apartment | Furnished | 2 beds, 2 baths
A modest shared apartment twenty minutes from the beach. Internet, water, and electricity included. This may be the way to go if you're on a strict budget. But of course, you must be cautious about choosing a roommate.

Potrero
$450/month | Furnished |1 bed, 1 bath | 400 sq. feet
Only a ten-minute walk to the beach, this ground-level apartment is located in a complex with a pool. At home, you're close to neighbors, but you won't be once you take that short walk to the beach. There you can stretch out and listen to the crashing waves.

Nosara (Guiones)
$550/month | Furnished | 2 beds, 1 bath | 600 sq. feet
Clean and furnished casita, only a half a mile to the nearest beach. It's 1.5 miles to the center of town, so you may want to consider having some form of transportation.

Tronadora
$500/month | Furnished | 2 beds, 2 baths | 700 sq. feet
"You can flush your toilet paper!" this ad proclaims. A beautiful casita overlooking Lake Arenal that not only offers an updated septic system but has hot water throughout. You can't ask for

more than that. If you're an artist, these views will inspire you to paint a masterpiece.

Nuevo Arenal

$350/month | Furnished | 1 bed, 1 bath | 400 sq. feet
A studio apartment. Nothing fancy, but suitable for one person.

Renting on a $2500 per Month Budget:
Moderately Appointed

Tamarindo

$750/month | Furnished | 1 bed, 1 bath | 753 sq. feet
This condominium is located only ten minutes from the beach in a complex with a pool. It features hot water throughout, and you can flush your toilet paper. Let the good times roll.

Potrero

$800/month | Furnished | 2 beds, 2 baths | 975 sq. feet
This newly renovated house is only two blocks from the beach, restaurants and supermarkets. Calling it a supermarket is probably a stretch. Many stores near the beach are small bodegas. But you will find most of what you need.

Nosara

$700/month | Furnished | 1 bed, 1 bath | 550 sq. feet
Lush landscaping surrounds this cute studio, and it's only 650 meters to the beach. Not luxurious, but being close to the sea surely makes up for amenities.

Tronadora

$1000/month | Furnished | 3 beds, 2 baths | 2100 sq. feet
This lake-view home is a beauty, with internet, granite countertops, and modern appliances. It doesn't have cable or satellite television, which is perfect if you plan on eliminating all the noise in your life. Why not binge-watch a show on Netflix? Or read a book. Or better yet, stare out at the lake and enjoy the view.

Nuevo Arenal

$750/month | Furnished | 2 beds, 2 baths | 1500 sq. feet
Nature surrounds this two-story home. With its lake view, it is quite the find. You will need transportation since it's a distance from the center of town, but at this price, there could be room in the budget for a car.

Renting on a $3500 per Month Budget: Gringo Style

Tamarindo

$2000/month | Furnished | 3 beds, 2.5 baths | 2100 sq. feet
This townhouse is modern and has a pool. You'll be close to your neighbors, and possibly noise. It's the trade-off for living in a touristy town.

Potrero

$2500/month | Furnished | 2 beds, 2 baths | 1900 sq. feet
Beachfront! This is a nicely appointed condo, and it has modern amenities. It even comes with a washer and dryer. You'll live like a king while listening to the tide roll in.

Nosara

$2000/month | Furnished | 3 beds, 2.5 baths | 1500 sq. feet
A beautifully appointed home on a hill with a pool. You'll need an SUV, especially during the rainy season.

Tronadora

$1200/month | Furnished | 2 beds, 2.5 baths | 1300 sq. feet
This lovely lake-view home features high-end appliances, teak wood throughout, cathedral ceilings, and an infinity pool. The backyard is a bird lover's dream.

Nuevo Arenal

$1500 | Furnished | 2 beds, 2.5 baths | 1200 sq. feet
A lake-view home with a lovely backyard. Nice appliances and high ceilings.

• •

Purchasing Real Estate: Under $150,000

Tamarindo

$120,000 | Unfurnished | 2 beds, 2 baths | 860 sq. feet
A well-appointed condominium, and it's only a five-minute drive to the beach. The complex includes a gym, rancho, and squash court.

Potrero

$149,000 | Furnished | 2 beds, 2 baths | 1070 sq. feet | Postage stamp acreage

Small home only steps from the beach. In a complex with a pool and tended landscaping, it's near other homes. If you don't mind the lack of privacy, this place is ideal.

Nosara

$135,000 | Furnished | 2 beds, 1 baths | 950 sq. feet | .05 acres
This listing features a bungalow-style home in a gated community. It includes a carport, stainless steel appliances, and a community pool. Although it's not walking distance to the beach, it is near a school.

Nuevo Arenal

$130,000 | Furnished | 4 beds, 3 baths | 1100 sq. feet | .3 acres
A Tico-style home in a quiet setting. The perfect place to get away from the rat race.

Tronadora

$80,000 | Furnished | 1 bed, 1 bath | 850 sq. feet | .4 acres
Private Tico style home near a river. Surrounded by trees and an abundance of wildlife.

Purchasing Real Estate: $150,000–$250,000

Tamarindo

$180,000 | Furnished | 3 beds, 2.5 baths | 1615 sq. feet | .88 acres
Just five minutes outside Tamarindo, this home has granite countertops and stainless steel appliances. It doesn't have a pool, but it's in a gated community. Oddly, they show an artist's rendering of a pool on their website with people playing

ecstatically in the water. Thanks, but may I respectfully suggest that most would rather have the *actual* three-dimensional pool full of non-ecstatic neighbors?

Potrero

$235,000 | Furnished | 2 beds, 2 baths | 1400 sq. feet | .15 acres
This immaculate home has stainless steel appliances, custom woodwork throughout, a security system, in-ground pool, and a stackable washer and dryer. The backyard doesn't have much landscaping, so it's perfect for those who don't have a green thumb or who want to start a garden from scratch. Only a five-minute walk to the beach and a nearby bodega.

Nosara

$169,000 | Furnished | 2 beds, 2 baths | 1076 sq. feet | .1 acres
A few minutes' drive to the beach, this home is appointed with stainless steel appliances and a stackable washer and dryer. There isn't much privacy from your neighbors, but it does have a security system.

Nuevo Arenal

$178,000 | Furnished | 2 beds, 2 baths | 1345 sq. feet | .4 acres
Beautiful home with hot water and woodwork throughout, high ceilings, granite countertops, and security system. Nice yard with fruit trees.

Tronadora

$160,000 | Furnished | 2 beds, 2 baths | 1075 sq. feet | .6 acres
Open-concept, lake-view home with granite countertops and stainless steel appliances.

Purchasing Real Estate: $250,000–$375,000

Tamarindo
$349,000 | Furnished | 2 beds, 2 baths | 1350 sq. feet
Beautiful ground-floor condominium with custom woodwork. A two-minute walk to the beach, and it has an outdoor bathroom off the bedroom. I once stayed in a hotel with that feature, and when I opened the door to use the bathroom in the middle of the night, the local bug committee was holding its annual convention. To get a good feel for what was happening, I flicked on the light, and all hell broke loose. Moral of this story is don't get up in the middle of the night to pee in an outdoor bathroom.

Potrero
$350,000 | Furnished | 3 beds, 2 baths | 1721 sq. feet | .13 acres
This house has an open-concept design with high ceilings, beautiful French doors, in-ground pool, and air conditioners in every room. Home has a wall around it and is protected by a security system with remote phone access capability. Only a five-minute walk to the beach.

Nosara
$319,000 | Furnished | 3 beds, 2 baths | 2500 sq. feet | 1.3 acres
Surrounded by the jungle, this house backs up to a nature preserve. It has an open kitchen and living area, a large balcony, and vaulted ceilings, and it's just minutes to the beach.

Nuevo Arenal

$350,000 | Unfurnished | 3 beds, 2 baths | 3000 sq. feet | 1.24 acres
A new home with high ceilings and panoramic windows to take in the views of the lake and volcano. High-quality appliances and tropical wood cabinets. This is great if you need a little extra space and some acreage. You can plant one heck of a garden here.

Tronadora

$300,000 | Furnished | 3 beds, 2 baths | 2800 sq. feet | .5 acre
Lovely home on the lake with a large deck for entertaining. Lots of details, with custom woodwork, granite countertops, security system including metal roll-down shutters, and a two-car garage.

Purchasing Real Estate: $375,000–$500,000

Tamarindo

$490,000 | Furnished | 3 beds, 3 baths | 2200 sq. feet
A modern second-story condominium with expansive views of the ocean. There are three balconies and a gourmet kitchen. The complex has a pool and 24-hour security. Only a five-minute walk to the beach.

Potrero

$400,000 | Unfurnished | 3 beds, 3.5 baths | 2690 | .12 acres
Beautiful two-story home with vaulted ceilings and custom woodwork. It seems to have it all except for a pool. This can be problematic if you plan on renting out the house. Most people want a pool, especially in a climate as hot as this.

Nosara

$450,000 | Furnished | 3 beds, 3 baths | 1400 sq. feet | .66 acres
This property has a pool, a rancho, and a two-car garage.
There's also a separate one-bedroom casita in the backyard and
extensive landscaping.

Nuevo Arenal

$425,000 | Furnished | 3 beds, 3 baths | 2400 sq. feet | .45 acres
This recently remodeled home features an incredible lake view,
beautifully landscaped yard with fruit trees, and an in-ground
pool.

Tronadora

$400,000 | Furnished | 3 beds, 2 baths | 1680 sq. feet | 3.5 acres
An incredible home overlooking Lake Arenal. High ceilings,
skylights, wrap-around veranda, and high-end appliances. It
features a 500 sq. foot garage for your tools and vehicles.

 ## Purchasing Real Estate: Over $500,000

Tamarindo

$990,000 | 4 beds, 3.5 baths | 3700 sq. feet
Two-story luxury condo with expansive ocean views. This
home features a state-of-the-art kitchen, high-end appliances,
spiral staircase, and arched doorways. It's only a three-minute
walk to the beach. The complex has a pool and tennis courts.

Potrero

$1.7 million | Furnished | 4 beds, 7 baths | 6200 sq. feet | .25 acres
You get everything with this listing: beachfront location, in-ground pool, outdoor kitchen, and a private entrance to every bedroom. It has marble countertops, vaulted ceilings, and a security system. The views of the ocean from the second floor are spectacular.

Nosara

$990,000 | Furnished | 4 beds, 4.5 baths | 3000 sq. feet | 1 acre
Balinese-style home with high-end finishings and an incredible pool. Located under a canopy of trees, this house is perfect for someone who wants indoor/outdoor living.

Nuevo Arenal

$600,000 | Furnished | 3 beds, 3.5 baths | 3100 sq. feet | 1.35 acres
A stunning lake-view home perfect for entertaining. The property is completely fenced in. It includes a one-car garage and is built to North American codes, featuring a large kitchen, barbecue area, and high-end finishes. A bonus one-bedroom casita on the property is perfect for guests or as a source of rental income.

House Hunting: Southern Pacific Coast

"Look to the future because that's where you'll spend the rest of your life."
~ George Burns

The following are average costs of renting or purchasing a home in Jacó, San Isidro de El General, Quepos, Dominical. A small description follows each listing and may help you decide if that price range is something you can live with. Due to copyright issues, I could not include pictures of each home, but after a quick search on the internet, you will find something similar (see chapter "Searching for Listings").

To use this chapter:
1. Decide whether you're renting or buying.
2. Pick one of the four towns.
3. Choose which category matches your budget.

Renting on a $1200 per Month Budget: Tico Style

Jacó

$550/month | Furnished | 2 beds, 1 bath | 720 sq. feet

This apartment is located in a complex with a pool. There is a suicide shower, but it's only a five-minute drive into town. It's near a bus stop, so it's perfect for someone on a budget that doesn't allow for a vehicle.

San Isidro de El General

$380/month | Unfurnished | 3 beds, 1 bath |1600 sq. feet

Just the basics. Clean and walking distance to town. You need not purchase a car with this rental, but you will need to buy furniture.

Quepos

$500/month | Furnished | 2 beds, 1 bath 650 sq. feet

A simple apartment with just the bare minimum. But it's furnished, so that's a plus.

Dominical

$600/month | Furnished | 1 bed, 1 bath | 750 sq. feet

A charming home nestled in the woods. It's a fifteen-minute drive to the beach. No bus stop nearby, so you will need transportation.

Renting on a $2500 per Month Budget:
Moderately Appointed

Jacó

$1000/month | Furnished | 2 beds, 2.5 baths | 1100 sq. feet
Ocean-view condo within walking distance of the beach. The complex has a pool and security.

San Isidro de El General

$700/month | Unfurnished | 3 beds, 2 baths | 1800 sq. feet
An incredible mountain-view home less than three miles from the center of town. It's on a quiet street and is the perfect place to enjoy cooler temperatures.

Quepos

$800/month | Furnished | 2 beds, 1 bath | 750 sq. feet
A bright furnished apartment only five minutes by car to Quepos. There's also a bus stop nearby. A washing machine is available at $5 per load.

Dominical

$750/month | Furnished | 2 beds, 1 bath | 1650 sq. feet
This rental doesn't come with air conditioning or washer and dryer. It's walking distance to the beach and public transportation, so you wouldn't need a car.

Renting on a $3500 per Month budget: Gringo Style

Jacó
$2400/month | Furnished | 3 beds, 2 baths | 2000 sq. feet
In the prestigious Los Sueños resort, this ocean-view condo is overflowing with luxury. Granite countertops, a gourmet kitchen, washer/dryer, and a balcony to enjoy gazing out at the passing sailboats. This resort has everything from a golf course to a fitness center.

Quepos
$1500/month | Furnished | 3 beds, 2 baths | 1500 sq. feet
A beautiful jungle-view home only a ten-minute drive from the center of town. It includes a washer/dryer, pool, air conditioning, and a large fenced-in backyard for pet owners. Perfect for someone who has just arrived in Costa Rica and needs a solid starting point.

San Isidro de El General
$1200/month | Furnished | 3 beds, 2 baths | 2200 sq. feet
A furnished home featuring granite countertops, stainless steel appliances, hardwood cabinets and doors, ceramic tile, carport, washer/dryer, and an on-demand gas water heater. Only 4.8 miles to the center of town and near a bus stop. Roads are paved, which will greatly reduce wear and tear on your car.

Dominical

$2100/month | Furnished | 2 beds, 3 baths | 2300 sq. feet
Beautiful villa on a ridge with incredible ocean views. A fifteen-minute walk into town and also near a bus stop.

• •

 ## Purchasing Real Estate: Under $150,000

Jacó

$68,000 | Unfurnished | 2 beds, 1 bath | 590 sq. feet
This Tico-style condominium doesn't have many amenities or high-end anything. But if you don't mind being very close to neighbors and don't want to invest much, this could be your place. It's close enough to the beach to walk, but you still may want to have transportation.

San Isidro de El General

$110,000 | Furnished | 2 beds, 2 baths | 1 acre
A Tico-style home with mature landscaping and a carport.

Quepos

$99,000 | Furnished | 2 beds, 2 baths | 855 sq. feet
You won't need a vehicle since this condominium is located right in town. Beautiful exotic hardwood floors throughout and granite countertops. The complex includes 24 hour security, a pool, and a barbecue area. One might consider this as a lower entry point in Costa Rica, with the possibility of renting it out for additional income when one isn't there.

Dominical

$125,000 | Furnished | 2 beds, 2 baths | 1290 sq. feet | 1.3 acres

This home is in a gated community and only a ten-minute drive to Dominical. Although not on a paved road, it has great mountain views and tons of wildlife. It's best to own an SUV since the rainy season can make a mess out of a dirt road.

 ## Purchasing Real Estate: $150,000–$250,000

Jacó

$225,000 | Furnished | 2 beds, 2 baths | 1022 sq. feet

In a gated community, this ocean-view condo has granite countertops, stainless steel appliances, washer/dryer, and access to a pool.

San Isidro de El General

$245,000 | Furnished | 9 beds, 6 baths | 5300 sq. feet | 2.75 acres

Located twenty-five minutes outside of San Isidro, this private mountain-view home is perfect for someone with a large family.

Quepos

$195,000 | Furnished | 4 beds, 2 baths | 1400 sq. feet | .08 acre

This side-by-side duplex does not have a pool but features gorgeous mountain views. It's within walking distance to the center of town. Each duplex has two bedrooms and two bathrooms, making it an income producer. You can live in one and rent the other!

Dominical

$199,000 | Furnished | 2 beds, 2 baths | 2400 sq. feet | 1.24 acres
A private mountain-view home fifteen minutes from Dominical, featuring its own access road, a large porch, and fruit trees. It's close to a waterfall, and this listing mentions the ASADA (water rights association). I haven't seen many that do this, so they know that a strong water association is a good selling point.

 ## Purchasing Real Estate: $250,000–$375,000

Jacó

$350,000 | Furnished | 3 beds, 3 baths | 2100 sq. feet | .05 acres
This two-story, oceanfront townhouse has a garage, balconies off each bedroom, an outdoor shower, and high-end appliances. Beautiful tile work, close to town, with access to the community pool.

San Isidro de El General

$349,000 | Furnished | 4 beds, 3.5 baths | 3100 sq. feet | 15 acres
Horse lovers—check it out! This country estate has a horse stable, tree plantation, two creeks, and panoramic views of the rolling hillside. The home features two levels with hardwood floors throughout. It also includes a caretaker's house.

Quepos

$329,000 | Furnished | 3 beds, 3 baths | 3500 sq. feet | .9 acres
Located six miles from Quepos, this country home offers incredible views of the forest. Although it doesn't include a garage, it has a bodega where you can store your tools.

Dominical

$330,000 | Furnished | 3 beds, 2 baths | 2200 sq. feet | 5 acres
Two-story mountain and ocean-view home with plenty of privacy. It features a one-car garage, a large porch, and a pool. Mature trees are already bearing fruit throughout the property. Only twelve minutes to the beach.

Purchasing Real Estate: $375,000–$500,000

Jacó

$488,000 | Furnished | 4 beds, 3 baths | 2200 sq. feet
Ocean-view condominium on the sixth floor. Wrap-around balconies make it an excellent place to listen to crashing waves. The complex has 24-hour security and a pool. Within walking distance of everything Jacó has to offer.

San Isidro de El General

$460,000 | Furnished | 5 beds, 4 baths | 4000 sq. feet | 25 acres
If you want to live on a large parcel of land, this property may be the one for you. It includes not only a guesthouse but a caretaker's house, a pool, and a wraparound deck. It's surrounded by mature landscaping and has wonderful views of the mountains.

Quepos

$480,000 | Furnished | 4 beds, 5 baths | 4000 sq. feet | 1.1 acres
A beautiful home in a gated community and only a ten-minute drive to the center of town. It features a saltwater pool, high-end appliances, granite countertops, jungle views, two-car car-

port, and high ceilings. One can easily imagine sitting in the backyard and watching the birds and monkeys overhead.

Dominical

$399,000 | Furnished | 2 beds, 2 baths | 2050 sq. feet | 10 acres
Mountain- and ocean-view home with ten acres of mature landscaping. The home also features a pool, guesthouse, and rancho. It's ideal if you're looking for extra income. You can rent the guesthouse while living in the main home. With this much land, you're surrounded by monkeys, toucans, anteaters, sloths, and parrots.

 ## Purchasing Real Estate: Over $500,000

Jacó

$1.2 million | Furnished | 4 beds, 4.5 baths | 4000 sq. feet
Oceanfront, two-story penthouse with floor-to-ceiling glass. It resembles a movie star's home in Malibu. It's oceanfront, so I would do my homework and inquire if it's within the Maritime Zone.

San Isidro de El General

$820,000 | Furnished | 5 beds, 4 baths | 4000 sq. feet | 55 acres
Located twenty minutes outside of San Isidro, this home is perfect for someone longing to be surrounded by wildlife. It features a gourmet kitchen, top-end appliances, a pool, rancho, barbecue area, and mature landscaping. And with all this acreage, you don't have to worry about noisy neighbors.

Quepos

$725,000 | Furnished | 4 beds, 5 baths | 3000 sq. feet | .4 acres

A beautiful eco-friendly estate in a gated community. Although nestled in the jungle, it also has an ocean view. Monkeys will spy from the tree above while you're swimming in the pool or lounging on the terrace. This home features top-of-the-line everything. Solar and wind power sources provide free energy to this home.

Dominical

$695,000 | Furnished | 4 beds, 4 baths | 9000 sq. feet | 14 acres

Amazing three-story ocean- and mountain-view home overstocked with luxurious features: vaulted ceilings, custom woodwork, a gourmet kitchen, private balconies, a rancho, and a pool. Surrounded by forest, you'll wake up to the sounds of birds and monkeys every morning.

House Hunting: Caribbean

"The life you have led doesn't need to be the only life you have."
~Anna Quindlen

Throughout all my research scouring for housing in Costa Rica, no other area was harder than the Caribbean. It was easier finding short-term rentals and vacation homes but challenging finding long-term rentals.

After talking with friends living in the Caribbean, they advised that it's best to have your feet on the ground when searching for rentals and property. Talk with realtors and business owners. Everyone knows of someone looking for a roommate or a tenant, and many of those listings are now in Facebook groups.

The following are average costs of renting or purchasing a home in Cahuita, Puerto Viejo, and Playa Chiquita. A small description follows each listing and may help you decide if that price range is something you can live with. Due to copyright issues, I could not include pictures of each home, but after a quick search on the internet. you will find something similar (see chapter "Searching for Listings").

> To use this chapter:
> 1. Decide whether you're renting or buying.
> 2. Pick one of the four towns.
> 3. Choose which category matches your budget.

 ## Renting on a $1200 per Month Budget: Tico Style

Cahuita

$550/month | Furnished | 2 beds, 1 bath | 860 sq. feet
Only a ten-minute drive to Cahuita, this Tico-style home has a carport, washer and dryer, and a yard. It is not near any bus stops.

Puerto Viejo

$300/month | Furnished Room for Rent | 1 bed, shared bath | 1050 sq. feet (shared space)
A furnished room in a home close to the beach and a bus stop. Sharing a home may be the best way to start for those on a very strict budget.

Renting on a $2500 per Month Budget : Moderately Appointed

Puerto Viejo

$675/month | Furnished | 1 bed, 1 bath | 800 sq. feet
This listing includes utilities, but there is no air conditioning. It doesn't have many of the amenities that homes in different parts of the country may offer.

Playa Chiquita

$700/month | Furnished | 2 beds, 2 bath | 850 sq. feet
A nicely appointed house with an alarm, roofed terrace, and hot water throughout. It's surrounded by mature trees so you'll enjoy watching the incredible wildlife while drinking your morning cup of coffee.

Renting on a $3500 per Month Budget: Gringo Style

Puerto Viejo

$1100/month | Furnished home | 2 beds, 2 baths | 1400 sq. feet
This home is nicely appointed, and you'll have access to a community pool, rancho, and gym. It also features 24-hour security.

Purchasing Real Estate: Under $150,000

Playa Chiquita
$85,000 | Furnished | 3 beds, 2 baths | 2150 sq. feet
A rustic home surrounded by nature. Close to the sea and near a bus stop.

Puerto Viejo
$125,000 | Furnished | 2 beds, 1 bath | 1200 sq. feet | .10 acres
A Tico-style home ten minutes to Puerto Viejo. It's close to the beach and a bus stop. It does not have air conditioning.

 ## Purchasing Real Estate: $150,000–$250,000

Puerto Viejo
$225,000 | Furnished | 2 beds, 2 baths | 1320 sq. feet | .25 acres
This home is near the beach and one mile from town. It has air conditioning in the master bedroom, high ceilings, its own well, and hot water on demand throughout.

 ## Purchasing Real Estate: $250,000–$375,000

Cahuita
$260,000 | Furnished | 4 beds, 2 baths | 3000 sq. feet | 1.25 acres
A two-story home close to the beach. It features a garage, pool, barbecue area, and an incredible garden of fruit trees.

Puerto Viejo

$299,000 | Furnished | 4 beds, 3 baths | 2800 sq. feet | .2 acres
Located less than two miles from Puerto Viejo, this listing is actually two Tico-style homes perfect for an investor. Live in one and rent out the other. Although basic, it does have a washer/dryer and on-demand hot water. There is no air conditioning.

 ## Purchasing Real Estate: $375,000–$500,000

Cahuita

$385,000 | Furnished | 3 beds, 1 bath | 1200 sq. feet
Rustic two-story home with an outdoor Jacuzzi. It has a beautiful ocean view and is only a short distance to a national park.

 ## Purchasing Real Estate: Over $500,000

Playa Chiquita

$850,000 | 4 beds, 3 baths | 3013 sq. feet | 1.2 acres
In a gated community, this home is steps away from a charming beach with natural sea pools, protected primary forest, abundant wild fauna, and good roads.

Puerto Viejo

$1.5 million | Multiple Furnished Homes | Main Home 2000 sq. feet
These five homes of various sizes are perfect for someone looking for an investment. All are nicely appointed and include air conditioning. This home has a pool and incredible jungle views.

Ramblings

I love the Caribbean coast and have had so much fun exploring the area. However, if you choose to live here, understand that it's less developed, so you won't have all the amenities you may be used to. The biggest complaint I hear from residents is that people didn't quite understand what that meant. They moved there, and instead of enjoying all the unspoiled nature around them, they found that it was difficult and they missed the amenities they enjoyed in more populated areas.

Could you imagine living here?

Creating a Budget

Four Budget Breakers

"If you think nobody cares if you're alive, try missing a couple of car payments."

~ Earl Wilson

Now that you have an idea of what a suitable home might cost you, we can go further into crafting a budget. There are significant start-up costs that need consideration. Not included in these budget-breaking start-up choices are extenuating circumstances, such as hard-to-find medications, healthcare needs, or work-related expenses.

Ask yourself these four questions before moving to Costa Rica:

- What form of transportation will you be using in Costa Rica?
- Will you be shipping your belongings?
- Do you plan on applying for residency?
- If you have children, do you plan to send them to school?

Method of Transportation

1. Purchasing a Car

If it's in your budget, I would recommend buying a car. With strong resale values, you should be able to sell it for a reasonable price if you decide to move back home. Once you shop for a vehicle, you may be surprised at how expensive they are in Costa Rica. This is because of import taxes applied to any car that will be in the country for over 90 days. Whether it's shipped or driven across the border, these vehicles are subject to an import tax.

Import Taxes based on Age of Vehicle
0–3 years — 52.29%
4–5 years — 63.91%
6+ years — 79.03%

As I have stated above, even if you drive your car across the border, as long as you plan on keeping the vehicle in Costa Rica, you'll pay a tax. There is absolutely no way of getting around it. And as you can see by these figures, shipping your 1995 Chevy Corolla will actually cost you more money than importing a newer car. Even Costa Rica doesn't want that piece of junk on the road. No offense.

So what are you going to pay? Generally, expats search for a used car around ten years old. That's the magic number. A car you would probably consider trading in when living in the United States is the one you'll gladly drop twelve grand for here. I would allocate twelve to sixteen thousand dollars for a reliable ten-year-old vehicle. New cars start at twenty-five grand and go up from there.

While shopping for a vehicle, chose a popular model. Labor is inexpensive, but parts are costly. That's if you can find them at all. If you buy a car that no one else in Costa Rica drives, you can expect to venture across the country like Hernán Cortés searching for a side mirror—a mirror required to pass inspection. If you can't get an inspection (at *Retive*), you can't get your car registered (your *marchamo*). And if you can't get your car registered, it will be impounded if driven.

"But I only budgeted five thousand dollars for a car!" you say. Well, you better budget five grand more for repairs because cars in that price range will come with many problems. It's possible to find a good deal, perhaps from an expat who is moving back home and wants to unload their car quickly. This could take years to come across, so I wouldn't count on that.

Many expats ship their cars even though it costs the same as buying one in Costa Rica. The advantage is that you will know the condition of the car, and there should be no surprises. Except if that car gets smashed up during shipping… surprise!

The biggest advantage of having your own transportation is that it may help you find cheaper rent. Homes off the beaten path, or nowhere near a bus stop, are typically less expensive, sometimes hundreds of dollars per month less expensive.

Without residency, you cannot get a Costa Rican driver's license. You can drive legally on your home country's license, but only for 90 days. You will then need to leave the country and renew your visa. Many expats just go over the Panamanian or Nicaraguan borders for an hour, get their passports stamped, and return.

2. Renting a Car

If you don't want to go through the hassle of purchasing a car, you can always rent one. Many rental agencies offer long-term contracts (over 90 days) ranging from twenty-five dollars a day on up. I like this idea. It gives you time to search for the perfect living arrangements. Many realtors will ask you to drive, so having a vehicle will come in handy. It also gives you time to search for a reliable car.

Check with the car rental agency and find out if you can start a long-term contract right out of the gate. It's not the most economical choice, but it offers freedom and gives you time to figure a few things out. It's also a lot of fun to explore the country on your own.

> Vamos Rent-a-Car offers long-term leasing. Check out their webpage for more information.

3. Purchasing a Scooter

Not interested in buying a car? How about a 125cc scooter with an emasculating girly hum? Have you ever driven one? My husband says it's fun. I wouldn't know because I tried and instantly fell sideways. My husband found me, and my girly hum, stuck between two bougainvillea bushes.

If you feel like putzing around town, this is the choice for you. You will certainly save a lot of money in gas. When we owned our Mitsubishi SUV, it cost eighty dollars to fill the tank.

Our scooter cost six dollars. Rob falling off the scooter and slicing his hand open cost seventy dollars at the medical clinic. All in all, we're still up.

He said we'd save money on gas.

Although scooters are economical, they can be challenging when grocery shopping. Below is a video showing how we did it. And this was when the sun was shining. Imagine doing it in the rain.

A new scooter will set you back about $1800. Helmets are approximately fifty dollars.

 Why did we buy a car and a scooter?

Rob and I quickly realized that more affordable rents were often down long dirt roads that crossed a stream. A 4x4 is the most practical way to get to these homes. To save money on gas, we purchased a scooter.

We hit the ground running the moment we moved here. Rob and I traveled throughout the country, even driving into Panama and Nicaragua. These were the best trips of our lives and made for some of our funniest stories. I can still remember getting caught in a downpour at La Paz Waterfall Gardens and driving all the way back to Grecia on our little scooter. It was so cold up in the mountains. I held my husband tight; while he absorbed the full wrath of the storm, his broad shoulders kept me warm and shielded me from the pelting rain.

No matter how you get around Costa Rica, take the time to explore hidden beaches, travel to the tip of a volcano, and spend an afternoon relaxing under a palm tree. Never pass up a long, winding dirt road. The best parts of Costa Rica are always at the end of one.

> Why did we purchase a used car this year that no one else in Costa Rica drives? A model that's impossible to find parts for and ignores all my own advice?
>
> Because we are idiots.

4. Using Public Transportation

Many expats use Costa Rica's extensive public transportation system. Although buses are very affordable, taxis are expensive, and Uber service is sketchy. The police have recently confiscated Uber drivers' license plates in San José, so it's unclear how this company will proceed in Costa Rica.

Addresses are not what you're used to, and it may take time for a taxi to find you. "Pick me up two hundred meters past the mango tree," you'll tell the driver. However, the mango tree won't be there anymore since it fell fifteen years ago during a storm. Remarkably, it's still your address.

Shipping Your Stuff or Starting Fresh

This is a very personal decision that only you can make. You may have belongings you want to take with you, and personal items you just can't part with. Or you simply love your cozy furniture. It's surprising how uncomfortable some couches and chairs are here.

If you choose to ship your things, there will be significant expenses. Please read my chapter "Barry the Shipper Extraordinaire" in *The Costa Rica Escape Manual 2019* for more information.

 Why did we start fresh?

For me, part of this process meant letting go of the past. I was on a quest to figure out why I was so unhappy. My existential crisis did not include holding on to wedding china or candlesticks. It did include Rob and my pets. And by getting rid of everything, it was as if I pushed away the life raft. It made me more determined to make things work.

Having a quick escape hatch makes it tempting to call it quits when times get hard. To prevent this from happening, we padlocked that door, nailed it shut, and then built a brick wall in front of the entrance. We needed an adventure, and we were going to give it the best shot of our lives to make it happen.

In retrospect, it was the best decision for us. Not being bogged down by our belongings gave us the freedom to move about with fewer hassles. Many if not most home rentals come furnished in Costa Rica, so we never needed those candlesticks after all.

Residency: Before, After or Never

1. Applying for Residency before Moving

Residency approval takes about one year from the date of submitting your application. There are horror stories about it taking much longer, and heroic ones where folks get theirs in just six months. But be aware that this process takes time and includes a good deal of paperwork (apostille-stamped birth certificate, marriage license, police report, etc.). It's easier to collect these documents while still living in your home country. Most are only valid for six months, and if you're late filing any one of them, immigration may deny the entire application.

Once you hand these documents over to your Costa Rican attorney, he or she will file your application with immigration, and in a few months you'll be "in the system." You won't get a cédula yet (your legal ID card). Instead, you'll be in limbo while waiting for final approval. Once you're in the system and your attorney has given you the okay, you will no longer need to leave the country every 90 days.

Once granted residency, you must contribute to the national health care system. That bill can start as high as two hundred dollars a month. As I stated earlier, you cannot get a

Costa Rican driver's license without a cédula (your legal ID card). You must continue to leave every 90 days to renew your visa so you can legally drive on your home country's driver's license.

2. Applying for Residency after Moving
You may want to test the waters before filing for residency. This will give you the chance to determine if this move is right for you without incurring the cost and hassle of applying for residency.

3. Never Apply for Residency at All
If you never apply for residency, you will always need to leave the country every 90 days. Some walk over the Panamanian or Nicaraguan border and return in an hour. If this sounds like you, consider living near either one of these borders. **This may determine the town in which you wish to live.**

Expats who leave every 90 days are referred to as *perpetual tourists*. I live in Guanacaste, and it's easy to travel from here to the Nicaraguan border, get your passport stamped, and return. But this will eventually become a hassle.

Although this is not illegal, it's technically not legal either. It's a gray area. But a nice gray area. Many have done it for years with no consequences. However, on some occasions, others were only given twenty days on their visa. When you're a perpetual tourist, you're at the mercy of the border agents. If you're standing in front of Priscila, and you look anything like her boyfriend, Gabriel, who just dumped her for her trampy cousin, you may be at that border for quite some time.

Rob and I were once stuck at the Panamanian border after the agent got annoyed and tossed my passport over his shoulder. I still have no idea why, since I thought I charmed him with my Spanglish. Heaven only knows what I might have said. The good news is that we made it out of there and Rob took this picture of me. See how I'm laughing in it? Old, grumpy office Nadine would have been angry. But I promised myself I would not screw up this amazing adventure, so instead I found the humor in it all. The new improved Nadine was emerging. I love looking back at these photos. It's a reminder that we are never lost but often stuck in the middle of two different worlds.

All Smiles

When did we apply for residency?

We applied after living in Costa Rica for a year. We really didn't think much about it since we were focused on leaving our jobs behind and starting a new life. Residency wasn't even on our radar. I'm still surprised at how little we knew and how far we've come.

Eventually, we didn't want to keep driving to Nicaragua or Panama. Typically expats visit border towns to make these runs quick and economical. We enjoyed Bocas del Toro the first five times we visited, but ultimately we wanted to be legal residents and contribute to the community. This is our home, and it was important to us that we were following the rules. At that time, you could get a Costa Rican driver's license without a cédula, so that had no bearing on our decision.

Private Schools

You can enroll your child in Costa Rican public school, but it's a Spanish curriculum. If you're considering English-speaking private schools, they can easily run over five hundred dollars a month. Many expats home school their children, so that's an affordable option.

Links
Vamos Rent-A-Car: vamosrentacar.com
Scooter shopping Video: youtu.be/e_CwUfFuzVw

Prices are in colones per kilo

Lifestyle

"At every party there are two kinds of people – those who want to go home and those who don't. The trouble is, they are usually married to each other."

~Ann Landers

How much does it cost to live in Costa Rica? If you're from San Diego, California, you may think it's quite affordable. If you are from Omaha, Nebraska, you may find it more expensive than you expected.

People will constantly argue about this on social media forums. An unsuspecting person asks a general question about expenses, and what follows are three hundred comments that only leave that person confused and wondering why there are so many grumpy people living in Costa Rica. This is because of something I learned a long time ago when Rob and I researched this move for ourselves. Few take the time to write the happy stuff, but angry folks can go on for hours.

Someone found a great deal at a farmers' market and came home with a week's worth of produce for only twenty dollars? No one will ever know because, instead of writing that, this individual complains that gas costs $4.50 per gallon. Someone had a great day at the beach and saw a turtle laying her eggs? That story is much less likely to show up in a forum than one about the astronomical price of Swiss cheese. I started Happier Than A Billionaire because it's only fair that people hear both sides of the story.

Just like anyplace else in the world, lifestyle will define cost of living in Costa Rica. Be honest with yourself and pinpoint the things you will sacrifice while defining the things you can't live without.

Hobbies

My friend loves to fish. He takes his kayak out every other day and enjoys time out on the water. He doesn't dine out often, drink, or smoke. His happy place is on the water and away from news channels and Instagram feeds. He just wants to breathe in that salty ocean air and catch a fish.

I have other friends who like to take part in art classes while others love to go to the movies.

What do you like to do? Surf, crochet, train for marathons, or shop for the latest fashions? Would you sacrifice any of it to move to Costa Rica?

Dining Out

Restaurants can be expensive in Costa Rica. There is a thirteen percent tax plus a ten percent gratuity added automatically to the bill. That always surprises people. A typical meal for two with a few alcoholic drinks can easily add up to over forty dollars. But there are also sodas (small Tico restaurants) where a similar meal may cost less than twenty dollars. These do not have all of the glamour of a fancier restaurant. There might even be a sleepy dog and rooster under your table. I've had incredible meals at these establishments, and they're a great way to dine out if you're on a budget.

Would you mind making more meals at home to save money?

Drinking and Smoking

I get many emails concerning the cost of liquor and beer in Costa Rica. Sometimes it can get heated. "A can of Imperial beer, which is made in Costa Rica, costs twenty cents more here than in the States!" one angry man proclaimed. Of all the questions to ask about moving to another country, this was his biggest concern.

I do not doubt the validity of this gentleman's grievance. It's probably true. Every country has its policies, and there are many items that are cheaper in the United States. For many, this may be a significant factor in their decision to move here. Below are prices on some popular items.

Cigarettes	
Pack of Marlboro Cigarettes	$3.80
Pack of Generic Cigarettes	$3.15
ALCOHOL	
1 liter Johnnie Walker Red	$32.85
750 ml Jack Daniels	$48.94
750 ml Jim Beam Bourbon	$30.86
750 ml Bacardi White Rum	$14.77
750 ml Baileys Irish Cream	$22.35
750 ml Absolut Vodka	$27.44
6 pack Imperial Beer	$7.67

Can you cut back on smoking and alcohol to tighten that budget if needed?

Driving a Car (one of my four budget-busting start-up costs)

In the chapters that follow, I give examples of real people's personal budgets. I did not include the cost of purchasing a car but did include the cost of gas, registration, insurance, and some repairs. If you do plan on purchasing a car, remember that with import taxes, it will cost twice as much as in the United States. Owing a car is a significant expense. If you are unlucky enough to get a lemon, repairs could eat up your entire budget.

But don't feel so bad. I just got off the phone with my husband's friend from Brooklyn, Tommy Walnuts. He was calling from New York Motor Vehicles to complain that he just forked over one thousand dollars for traffic violations. I'm assuming he paid them because there was a warrant out for his arrest. One can never be sure of Tommy's motivations. This will most likely not happen to you while living in Costa Rica. I haven't driven through one town that has cameras on any of their traffic lights. But police will ticket you for not wearing a seat belt or failing to register your car.

Can you afford to purchase a car? If not, are you comfortable taking public transportation?

Getting or Not Getting Residency (one of the four budget busting start-up costs)

If you are not getting residency, you will need to leave the country every 90 days to renew your visa. In reality, if you hop across the Panama or Nicaragua border, that trip may not cost all that much. In Guanacaste, you can take a shuttle for $45/person. Even though many people do this, I can say from personal experience this starts to get old. On the flip side, if you get residency, you will not have to make these trips, but you will have to contribute the Caja system.

> If you don't have residency, are you prepared for the 90 day visa run? If you get residency, are you prepared for the added Caja expense?

Pets

The good news is that veterinary care is reasonably priced. The bad news is that high-quality food is expensive. For example, my cat is a foodie with epicurean taste buds. She has declared in writing she will no longer eat her twenty-eight-dollar-per-bag Science Diet food. As of today, she is only consuming wet food, chicken breast, and anything we're eating at the moment. A can of wet food costs $1.25, and she eats four cans a day. She doesn't seem concerned that my weekly grocery bill just went up by thirty-five dollars. Do you want to quickly separate the gringos from the Ticos? Look for the lunatics who have an entire grocery cart full of Fancy Feast.

> Are your pets part of this move? Have you allotted money for the added expenses?

Utilities

This is a big one, guys. If you live near the coast, it will be hot. Some parts of the season are cooler than others, but you will likely be running your air conditioner at some point. For a modest home, if you use it frequently, your bill can easily be two hundred dollars a month. Add a pool and a few bedrooms and that cost can easily double. But we will talk with a couple using solar power and see how they are faring.

Would you be willing to live in a cooler area away from the beach if it meant a decrease in expenses?

Real People with Real Budgets

Manuel's Budget

"Until you value yourself, you won't value your time. Until you value your time, you will not do anything with it."

~ M. Scott Peck

If you like to surf more than work, then Manuel could be your life coach. He is thirty-four years old, married, and a freelance web designer. With an internet connection, he can work from anywhere, but that's on the days he's not battling some righteous waves in Tamarindo.

Manuel is Costa Rican but has lived in Chicago most of his life. After getting married, he and his wife moved to Costa Rica.

"We wanted a simpler life," he said. "The rat race was getting to us. We were working more and more and not spending any quality time with each other. We just thought, hey, let's get out of here and redefine our priorities."

Although it didn't make the most financial sense to leave in their thirties, Manuel was confident he would have enough freelancing jobs to stay afloat. After living in Tamarindo for a year, they found someone renting out a one-room casita. The owner basically needed a house sitter to make sure no one broke in or vandalized the property. You can't leave a house empty here for long before everything starts to disappear.

There were many problems with the house. Water wasn't reliable, the electric was shoddy, but the rent was perfect: $100/month. He was also just a mile from the beach.

"I'm not going to lie. We're on a tight budget. We don't eat out much or go out drinking. There's no money for that. The place we live has its issues. Some days we don't have water, other days it comes out of the faucet as a trickle. But we've traded those luxuries for our freedom and we've never been happier."

Manuel's Monthly Budget

Rent (studio, 1 bath)	**$100.00**

Automobile	
Insurance (additional private ins. above the mandatory marchamo)	0.00
Marchamo	27.00
Fuel (Diesel)	40.00
Retive (car inspection, $26.40 divided by 12)	2.20
Service and Repairs	25.00
Total	**$94.20**

Home	
Cleaning Services	0.00
Home Insurance	0.00
Homeowner's Ass.	0.00
Landscape & Maintenance (no pool)	0.00
Misc. Lawn and Garden (plants, tools)	0.00
Real Estate Tax	0.00
Repair & Maintenance (services, materials)	0.00
Security	0.00
Total	0.00

Utilities	
Electric	110.00
Propane	0.00
Water	25.00
2 Cell Phones	20.00
Internet	30.00
Cable	50.00
Total	**$235.00**

Entertainment	
Dining Out	25.00
Media (Netflix, Hulu, etc.)	15.00
Total	**$40.00**

Groceries	
Beer, Wine, Liquor	65.00
Food	425.00
Total	**$490.00**

Pets (no pets)	$0.00

Medical	
Doctor Visits	0.00
Caja Ins. (2 people)	150.00
Total	**$150.00**

Manuel's Total Monthly Budget	$1109.20

Manuel's Advice

"You're going to have to give up many comforts if you want to live on a lower budget like we do. Don't count on a house-sitting gig or finding a special deal on rent right away. These opportunities come along once you meet people and make friends and have been here a while.

"But if you really want to do this, I'd say go for it. Make a plan and see if you can design a whole new life here in Costa Rica. My wife and I may not stay forever, but for now we're having a blast. I surf in the morning, catch up on freelance work in the afternoon, and get to spend time with the love of my life. Who could ask for more than that?"

Maria's Budget

"The only person you are destined to become is the person you decide to be."
~Ralph Waldo Emerson

Maria is Costa Rican but moved to California when she was a teenager. She met her husband, Kevin, at work and they were both living the American dream. But high-stress jobs were taking a toll on their health, so they took early retirement. It's no secret that California is an expensive place to live, so they headed back to Maria's birthplace—back to Costa Rica.

They bought a home thirty minutes outside of Jacó and decided to install solar panels. The temperature of the southern Pacific zone is hot, and Maria was all too aware of the cost of electricity in Costa Rica. She knew they would use air conditioning, and electric would be one of their biggest expenses.

"We have solar panels, but no batteries, and a solar water heater," Maria explains. "If you choose to live in a hot and humid area as we do, I recommend acclimating to the weather as soon as you can. Try only turning on your air conditioning for short periods of time. Use ceiling fans as much as possible, or install solar panels, as electricity is one of the most expensive utilities. This bill can quickly get out of hand. Our solar panels even charge the electric golf cart we use for local trips. The alone has saved us an average of about sixty dollars a month in fuel.

"If you don't have solar panels, I also recommend switching to a propane stove. That's another way to cut your electric bill."

Maria points out that cost of living varies significantly no matter what country you're in. Things that seem super cheap in Costa Rica to a Californian like her husband may appear expensive to someone from Idaho. Compare the cost of where you're living now to different areas of Costa Rica before moving.

Maria's Monthly Budget

Automobile	
Insurance (additional private ins. above the mandatory marchamo)	103.83
Marchamo	40.00
Fuel	3500
Retive (car inspection, $26.40 divided by 12)	2.20
Service and Repairs	25.00
Total	**$206.03**

Home	
Cleaning Services	100.00
Home Insurance	22.60
Homeowner's Ass.	0.00
Landscape & Maintenance (no pool)	26.00
Misc. Lawn and Garden (plants, tools)	5.00
Real Estate Tax	29.16
Repair & Maintenance (services, materials)	166.66
Security	100.00
Total	**$449.42**

Utilities	
Electric (with panels minus batteries)	35.00
Propane	16.66
Water	29.41
2 Cell Phones	40.00
High Speed Internet /Cable TV/ Landline Phone	130.00
Total	**$251.07**

Entertainment	
Dining Out	300.00
Media (Netflix, Hulu, etc.)	20.00
Total	**$320.00**

Groceries	
Beer, Wine, Liquor	100.00
Food	600.00
Total	**$700.00**

Pets (1 large dog, 2 cats)	
Veterinarian	50.00
Dog Food	125.00
Total	**$175.00**

Medical	
Dentist	4.16
Caja Insurance (2 people)	100.00
Private Medical Insurance	0.00
Total	**$104.16**

Maria's Total Monthly Budget	$2205.68

Property Taxes

"In California, we lived in an older 1000--square-foot home. Our property taxes were $7500 a year, and we had a twenty-five-year mortgage. Our home in Costa Rica is almost triple the size, we are completely debt-free, and our property taxes are only $350 a year. There is nothing better."

Water Issues

"We live in a rural area and our current water supply is not potable. Therefore, AYA (government water entity) cannot charge the traditional rate without making further repairs to the system. At the moment they can only legally charge us $4.40 a month for water. At first this forced us to buy bottled water, which became expensive.

"Since then, we have installed a water filtration system that includes a UV filter that enabled us to make our own clean, drinkable water. We spend an average of $150 every six months on replacing filters and maintenance for this filtration system. Our water is $53 a year for AYA. It's important when looking for a place to live to access the quality and cost of water in that particular region."

Groceries and Dining Out

"We spend about $600 a month on groceries, but that's because my husband likes to eat well. I cook Chinese, Indian, Italian, French, Mexican, Costa Rican and fusion cuisine. If we had to cut back, we could bring that down to $350 a month.

"Keep in mind we accomplish this by smart shopping. I purchase items in bulk and utilize my freezer. By doing this I estimate saving 30–50%. I purchase fruits, vegetables, and herbs at the weekly farmers' market. I haggle on prices with vendors and they offer a large variety of organic and fresh items. I buy organic eggs from a local farmer that delivers them weekly to my home. When I want fish, I talk to the local fisherman and pick their catch of the day at a third of the price I would normally pay at the store.

"Our proteins include: chicken, pork, beef, and seafood. My vegetarian neighbor spends about $250 a month on food for two people buying everything at the farmers' market."

Maria's Advice

"Both my husband and I were suffering from quite a few medical ailments when we lived in California. Since moving to Costa Rica, they have either disappeared or decreased. Today we eat natural foods and have a more holistic approach to health. Being surrounded by nature is a healer to both mind and soul.

"But people need to understand that if they have baggage, like emotional problems, or if they are inherently grouchy, moving to a different country will not make all the bad things in life disappear. If anything, they might complicate things even more."

Stephen and Jackie's Budget

"Happiness is holding someone in your arms and knowing you hold the whole world."
~ Orhan Pamuk

Stephen and Jackie are a married couple in their early sixties who rent a small house in Potrero, Guanacaste. They are originally from Austin, Texas, and Stephen has been a professional musician most of his life. Although they resemble an average couple, they had a few rough years before moving to Costa Rica.

Jackie was diagnosed with colon cancer four years ago and went through extensive surgeries, radiation, and chemotherapy. Their life was turned upside down, with Stephen caring for his wife and responsible for much of her care. This involved scheduling Jackie's medical appointments and talking with doctors. "My only goal at that time was to get her better," he said.

Stephen spent hours on the phone with cancer facilities, getting transferred to one extension to the next. "I couldn't even get the secretary's secretary on the phone," he criticized. "There were times I had to go down to their office just to ask a question."

After all the treatments, Jackie's cancer was cured. That's when they started thinking about moving abroad. They both needed extensive dental work, and medical care in general was half the price it was in the United States.

"I came down with dentures, now I have a full set of implants," Stephen said.. They traveled all around the country, staying at different Airbnbs. After reading my books, they decided to head to Sugar Beach, one of my favorite places to write about.

"It was warm, quiet, and I thought this area was a good place to rent for six months," he said. "From there we would play it by ear." They've been here for over two years, and we've become good friends.

Jackie is now under the care of local doctors, and she is pleased with the attention she gets. "I have not used Caja for my doctor visits since it's so affordable to pay for private care. But I do plan to use Caja for any catastrophic emergencies."

Jackie had an endoscopy, which only cost her $130. Her doctors spent a lot of time with her and even gave their email so she could follow up with any questions. It was a completely different experience than in the United States.

Stephen and Jackie's Monthly Budget

Rent (2 beds, 2 bath, near beach)	$1000.00

Automobile

Insurance (additional private ins. above the mandatory marchamo)	0.00
Marchamo	25.00
Fuel	80.00
Retive (car inspection, $26.40 divided by 12)	2.20
Service and Repairs	75.00
Total	**$182.20**

Home

Cleaning Services	100.00
Home Insurance	0.00
Homeowner's Ass.	0.00
Landscape & Maintenance (includes pool)	130.00
Misc. Lawn and Garden (plants, tools)	0.00
Real Estate Tax	0.00
Repair & Maintenance (services, materials)	0.00
Security	0.00
Total	**$230.00**

Utilities

Electric	200.00
Propane	0.00
Water	11.00
2 Cell Phones	10.00
Internet	30.00
Cable	50.00
Total	**$301.00**

Entertainment

Dining Out	80.00
Media (Netflix, Hulu, etc.)	15.00
Total	**$95.00**

Groceries

Beer, Wine, Liquor	0.00
Cigarettes (Stephen)	114.83
Food	600.00
Total	**$714.83**

Pets (no pets)	**$0.00**

Medical	
Doctor Visits (Jackie)	50.00
Caja Ins. (2 people)	60.00
Total	**$110.00**

Manuel's Total Monthly Budget	**$2633.03**

 Stephen and Jackie's Advice

"People need to understand they may not have everything they had back home. For instance, we haven't found good Mexican food or the ingredients to make it. I bring spices down when I visit the States or I ask friends to bring them for me.

"You can forget about ordering anything online. It took me a year and a half to figure out where to buy the things we desired. Even though we rent a furnished house, we still have had to acquire a ton of kitchen things and other household items to make it livable for us long-term. We aren't buying much of anything like that anymore because we have everything we need now. People moving here might want to budget some money for those kinds of things."

Pete's Budget

"A man travels the world over in search of what he needs and returns home to find it."
~George A. Moore

When Rob and I lived in Grecia, we'd ride our scooter through Atenas on our way to the southern Pacific beaches. Atenas is in the Central Valley and is an excellent spot if you don't want to live too far from the beach; Jacó is only an hour and twenty minutes away. Atenas is also less than an hour from San José.

Our friend Pete lives there, and he has been one of the best resources for gathering information on budgeting in Costa Rica. He can rattle off all sorts of figures, whether it's the cost of his electric bill, the price of dining out, or even how many miles he gets out of his car's tires. And you can count on one thing: he will sugarcoat none of it.

Pete and his wife lived in Nashville, Tennessee, for seventeen years after moving from Detroit in 1990. After thirty-five years in the tire industry, he is now retired. Pete's idea of retirement did not involve staying in Nashville. He wanted to head south in search of a new adventure.

He first visited Mexico, but it wasn't the perfect place for him. When he returned to Nashville, Pete had dinner with a colleague and his wife, the latter having been born in Costa Rica. "Why don't you check out Costa Rica?" she asked. "It's a beautiful country."

As per her suggestion, he came down to Costa Rica and knew right away this was the place he would call home. His buddies thought he was nuts and even took bets on whether his wife would move with him. Once she visited, she too fell in love with this country and its people. Some of Pete's friends lost quite a bit on that wager.

He arrived in Atenas in 2007 and has never looked back. He has built two homes and is the proud owner of two dogs. The first stray he adopted had been hanging around the construction site of his first Atenas home. Pete named her Goofus because she was always getting into trouble. He renamed her later to Terrorist because she roamed the neighborhood, causing trouble with other dogs and cats. He finally settled on Abby. She is now twelve years old and has been the best dog he has ever owned. During the building of his new home, he adopted another stray. Vida is part German shepherd and is a little less than a year old. Unfortunately, Abby will not tolerate Vida playing with her. Once the top dog, always the top dog

Pete's Monthly Budget

Automobile	
Insurance (additional private ins. above the mandatory marchamo)	0.00
Marchamo	27.97
Fuel	236.18
Retive (car inspection, $26.40 divided by 12)	2.20
Service and Repairs (in a stroke of bad luck, Pete needed hefty repairs on his car this year)	365.35
Total	**$631.70**

Home	
Cleaning Services	258.30
Home Insurance	30.28
Homeowner's Ass.	70.00
Landscape & Maintenance (includes pool)	164.74
Misc. Lawn and Garden (plants, tools)	64.16
Real Estate Tax	87.98
Repair & Maintenance (services, materials) *new home still being tuned in	359.87
Security	31.30
Total	**$1066.63**

Utilities

Electric	210.54
Propane	12.96
Water	31.34
Cell Phones	135.38
High Speed Internet	65.03
Total	**$463.53**

Entertainment

Dining Out	287.71
Media (Netflix, Hulu, etc.)	9.15
Total	**$296.86**

Groceries

Beer, Wine, Liquor	252.55
Food	311.38
Supplies	89.23
Total	**$653.16**

Pets (2 dogs)

Veterinarian	24.97
Dog Food	50.00
Total	**$74.97**

Medical	
Dentist	21.87
Doctor	15.97
Medications	247.64
Caja Insurance	59.32
Private Medical Insurance (spouse only)	124.91
Total	**$469.71**

Pete's Total Monthly Budget	**$3656.56**

Building

"Building costs for the last home in Nashville, Tennessee, were $239 per square foot. I have learned I can build a new home in Atenas for between $62 and $63 per square feet. Today we have a main house, a two-apartment guest house, a rancho, and a pool on 1.81 acres in a gated community. The main house alone consists of 3200 square feet, and total construction cost us only $50,000 more than what we sold our 2300 square foot condominium in Brentwood, Tennessee."

Gated Communities

"HOAs are not legal in Costa Rica for single-dwelling homes. Many people who are aware of this refuse to pay any dues, which will have a negative impact on community services such as security and maintenance. To overcome this situation, as the then president of my last community, I had a service corporation formed, which became responsible for handling our front gate, security, and maintenance. The theme was 'no pay, no service. Open the gate yourself.'

"It wasn't long before we had all but one resident contributing monthly service fees. With a service corporation, you have the same ability as ICE (electric company) to refuse service for a lack of payment."

 Pete's Advice

"You must learn to adapt and change if you plan on moving to Costa Rica. There are many, many Americans who move here and end up going back, usually within a year. Based on what I have seen, expats arrive and expect everything to be the same as it is in the States for half the price.

"In essence, one must come here with an open mind and be willing to make adjustments. Our attitude regarding the language was that this is their country and their language. It's much better to show respect and at least try to speak their language."

Bonus Chapters from the
Costa Rica Escape Manual
2019

Building Your Home

My Husband: "We need more windows."
Me: "No. No, we do not."

There are some amazing homes in Costa Rica. Some with open courtyards revealing tropical gardens, and others with walls of glass built on mountaintops. The views are astounding, even in the most unremarkable places.

I remember walking through a mechanic's garage and finding a sweeping view of the Central Plateau in the rear of his building.

"Wow," I said.

"I love my country," the mechanic replied before he rolled himself underneath a car.

It's no wonder everyone's mind races when visiting, dreaming about whether they too can build a home here and start living the pura vida life. And you can if you do a little research and fully understand the practicalities of construction in a foreign country. Expect some surprises.

We've lived in a variety of houses around the country and found faulty electric, missing roof tiles, pipes that lead nowhere, and doors that open in the wrong direction. A common problem is improperly ventilated sewer pipes. That one is the worst! We knew when we built our home that we would have to find a competent builder, one who had many houses already under his belt. (You can read more about that hilarious year in *Happier Than A Billionaire: An Acre in Paradise*.)

If at all possible, it's best to be in Costa Rica so you can oversee the building process. I know a few people who built their homes while they were out of the country, only to return and find rooms that were too small or finishings that they never chose. These mishaps are not always due to a sinister contractor. Anytime you're dealing with different systems of measurements, unreliable utilities, and a language barrier, all from three thousand miles away, you can pretty much count on a hilariously tragic story or two. So please, supervise your construction so you don't return to find an Olympic-sized swimming pool and learn that you are now sixty million dollars over budget.

Building costs vary greatly depending on the style of finishes you choose and where you plan to build. Quotes range from $60 a square foot when building closer to San José, in places such as Grecia, to $80 to $150 per square foot if you're building near the beach. One reason things are more expensive at the beach is because of high fuel costs. The farther you are from San José, the more you'll pay for building materials.

Deciding whether to buy a house already built or to undergo the tedious process of constructing one will not be easy. However, purchasing an existing home will likely cost significantly more than building one yourself. It boils down to finances and how much energy you want to put into the project. If you decide to build, make sure you have the tenacity to see it through.

The Architect

The first step, and one that is required by law, is to hire an architect and engineer. I recommend you use one licensed by the Costa Rica Association of Engineers and Architects (Colegio Federado de Ingenieros y Arquitectos, also known as CFIA). Only a licensed architect can submit your plans to the municipality. The CFIA sets a minimum fee schedule, but there is no cap on how much one can charge.

One architect I recommend is José Pablo Acuna Lett, because he has been working with clients from the USA, Canada, the UK, France, Germany, and Russia for over ten years. He's also the architect that designed The Happier House! José was gracious and answered a few questions to help us better understand the process of designing a home in Costa Rica.

What is the first thing a foreigner should look for in an architect?

"When a foreigner is looking for an architect in Costa Rica, there are some important things to consider. Education is important. I studied at Tecnológico de Monterrey, a well-known university in Mexico, and I received my MBA specializing in international business. I travel a lot, and this exposes me to the many different building styles all around the world.

"If a person is not very confident with the Spanish language, communication will be easier with an English-speaking architect. It's a good idea to hire one who is knowledgeable about the area where you want to build and has experience. Always make sure your architect is a member of the CFIA."

What are the fees?

"The architectural, electrical, mechanical, structural, and A/C engineers charge a total of 10.5% of the projected building cost of the home," José explains. "This 10.5% is broken down into the following categories: 1.5% for preliminary studies and architectural design, 4% for architectural, electrical, plumbing, structural, A/C building plans and specifications, and 5% for site supervision by all professionals involved in the process during the time of construction."

What qualities make a good architect?

"I like to understand each client's needs and dreams. From the moment I meet a new client (in person or by email), I pay close attention to what they have in mind. Once I have a thorough understanding of their idea, I start the creative process. I always respond to a client's question or concern within twenty-four hours.

"I love all different types of architectural styles and have designed and built projects in Playas del Coco, Tamarindo, Playa Grande, Bay of Pirates, Conchal, Flamingo, Santa Teresa, and Punta Leona."

Where is your favorite place to build?

"Guanacaste has a special place in my heart. My parents brought me to Playas del Coco for the first time when I was four weeks old. It's always been my dream to be an architect in this area. I'm living my dream now, practicing my career in this paradise.

"Ecology and sustainable development are very important to me. I love working with alternative energy sources and bioclimatic architecture. I try to establish a good relationship with my clients beyond work to catch their essence and express it in the homes I design. Even though professional fees may not vary a lot from one architect to another (the CFIA sets a minimum fee schedule but there is no cap on how much one can charge), I always give my clients the very best deal I can. Living and working in the same area makes it easier for me because I don't have to charge for extra for travel expenses."

Are you familiar with the permit process in Guanacaste?

"I'm familiar with nearly every development in the area and have been personally involved with many. I have a strong understanding of Costa Rican bureaucracy, and this helps to move things along when applying for permits."

It's common for documents to get lost on someone's desk or be submitted to the wrong office. José makes sure that everything gets filed so that you don't find out five years down the line that you never officially had a building permit to begin with. A friend of mine is now facing this exact problem, and the amount of time it takes to rectify it is unbelievable.

The Builder

It's safe to say your Costa Rican home will be built using very strict earthquake codes. Our last major earthquake in Guanacaste was a doozy (7.6 on the Richter scale). It lasted for over a minute, and it felt like the house was exploding around us. It shook so much I couldn't even get our key into the metal gate at our front entrance. Finally, Rob pulled the keys out of my hands and was able to unlock it. Experts say not to run out of the house, since you're more likely to get killed by things falling on your head if you're outdoors. But our instincts told us to run... so we did. I'm surprised I didn't fall into a hole on the way out. I was a hysterical mess. I thought all my friends were dead, buried beneath a ton of rubble. Then there was the tsunami warning, which capped off the ultimate crappy days.

Before this episode, I always wondered if a big earthquake would expose inferior construction here like it often does in other countries around the world. Would we find newspaper stuffed into supporting columns, or a lack of rebar in concrete foundations? Thankfully, that didn't happen in Costa Rica. I feel much safer than I did before, and I'm confident that at the very least, most houses here have solid foundations.

I contacted our builder, Aaron, to hear his thoughts on construction.

What types of contracts are common with builders?

"A clear and solid contract with your builder is a great place to start," he says. "There are two common types of contracts: a line-item contract and a fixed-price contract. Let me explain the difference.

"In a line-item contact, the cost of labor is based on a percentage of the cost of your materials. The total cost of your project will be materials plus the agreed-upon percentage for labor. A fixed-price contract is exactly what it sounds like: the builder gives you one upfront price for the entire build.

"They both have advantages and disadvantages. One risk you take when choosing a line-item contract is that the cost of materials can fluctuate throughout the build, making it hard to predict the exact cost of the total project. The advantage of a fixed-price contract is that the client knows exactly what the home will cost. However, when creating a fixed-cost contract, builders will consider unforeseen circumstances. An estimated rising material cost will be factored into the quote, and all of this will usually lead to a higher price in the end."

Which do most prefer?

"Most of my clients prefer a line-item contract, as do I. If you have a good trusting relationship with your builder, this is usually the way to go. It's always a good idea to show up at the building site often in order to keep track of quality and the materials going into the project.

"Another important thing to consider is the climate in which you are building. A good design should have lots of cross ventilation and a good plan for outdoor living. Keeping radiant heat off a house is critical, and a lot of that can be accomplished with intelligent landscaping."

What are the most common building materials?

"There are three common ways most people choose to build in Costa Rica: concrete block, concrete/Styrofoam block, or steel stud. My clients can choose any of these, but I prefer steel because it goes up much faster and has an insulation rating of an R19. Concrete/Styrofoam block has an R19 insulation rating as well, but it's labor intensive and costs 20% more. Regular concrete block has a very poor insulation rating, so I'd rather not use it. Electricity is expensive in Costa Rica; it's critical that a house is well insulated in order to keep air conditioning costs down.

"I also favor steel because it's economical, better for the environment, creates less waste, and is not as cumbersome. It's easier to make adjustments or remodel later as well. For example, if you want to run a simple electrical line for another outlet, it's easy when using steel. If you have a house made of concrete block, it's much more time-consuming and expensive.

"I love my job and enjoy helping people build their dream homes. Having a good relationship with your builder is essential. I hate to say that I've seen some crazy stuff: retaining walls have been built out of roof tin, and drainage has been installed sending water back up against a house. Something very common in Costa Rica is plumbing being installed without proper ventilation. This will cause sewage gases to build up in the home, which smells terrible and can even become a health hazard. Always interview your builder, as well as his clients. A good builder will have no objection to letting you tour his projects."

Closing Costs

I reached out to a well-respected San José attorney, Alejandro Montealegre, for information regarding closing costs.

What terms will a contract have in regard to these costs?

"The law stipulates that, unless otherwise agreed by the parties, or legal disposition in contrary, the notary fees, registry fees, stamps and taxes, shall be paid by both parties (buyer and seller) in equal shares (50/50) except mortgages and their cancellations, which correspond 100% to the debtors.

"This means that, for example, ACME developer agrees to pay 50% of the notary fees of the mortgage, in case I'm appointed to be the notary authorizing the deed. If buyers are paying in cash for the property and decide to hire their own attorney-notary to draft the deed of transfer, buyers are responsible for paying 100% of the closing costs, except for my fees, which are paid separately by ACME. When part of the price of the purchase is financed by ACME, then ACME has the right to appoint me as the notary to draft the deed of transfer and the mortgage. In that case, ACME pays 50% of transfer fees, and buyers shall pay the remaining transfer fees, along with any fees for a mortgage, all transfer taxes, registry fees, and stamps of the deed."

Luxury Tax: This tax is to be paid by people who own residential properties in Costa Rica with a total value of approximately $229,600.00 USD or higher. The value of a property is determined by taking into account the value of the main construction plus the value of all permanent installations (pool, patio, etc.). If this value exceeds the amount mentioned above, then the cost of the land must be calculated and added to the value. This tax starts at a minimum of .25% for properties of up to $574,940.00 USD and in increments of 0.05%, with a max of 0.55% for properties whose value exceeds an approximate $3,458,540.00 USD.

Links

Aaron the Builder: acberkowitzmv@gmail.com

Ale Elliot, Mar Vista Project Manager:

www.marvistacr.com

Architect: José Pablo Acuna Lett, MBA

JPA Architecture and Planning

Email: jpalett@gmail.com

Tele: 2271-1965 Cell: 8830-4827

Costa Rica Association of Engineers and Architects:

www.cfia.or.cr

The Water Letter

"If my ship sails from sight, it doesn't mean my journey ends, it simply means the river bends."
~ Enoch Powell

It is imperative that water distribution to your home and/or project is legal. Brett, from the previous chapter, helped shed light on the various ways of obtaining legal water. And by legal, I mean that the developer has the right to deliver water to each parcel within the project. It's something that most people are not aware of before purchasing land, and it can be the difference between fulfilling your dream and losing your money.

Costa Rica is the legal owner of all water, and even mineral rights below the soil. Just because there is water on your property does not mean it's legal to use it. Even if PVC pipes are running to your lot and the seller says, "Look, just turn on the faucet, and you have running water!" that does not guarantee any of it is legal.

Different Concessions Granted to Access Water

Legally Registered Artesian Well (Hand-Dug) This type of concession is only meant for agricultural and uni-residential purposes. It's a legal water system for only one farmhouse on one farm. It is illegal for this landowner to distribute water to areas outside the boundaries of his farm or to multiple properties cut from the mother farm. Although legal, it's the least favorable concession.

It's not uncommon to come across a seller who has subdivided his land into smaller parcels and claims he can legally provide water to each lot. You need to check if the seller has the right not only to pump water from this well but also to distribute the water to others. Request this proof in writing, and have your attorney double-check the authenticity against the public records at AYA in San José.

If you buy an existing home with this water setup, there is some risk. If buying a piece of property with the intent of building on it, you are at extreme risk of never getting a building permit.

Neighborhood Usage Association A group of neighbors get together and have concession rights to one well (either artesian or machine-dug). This group is responsible for maintaining water quality and the infrastructure needed to distribute water. This type of association, while not the strongest form of water rights, is usually tolerated and grandfathered in if the neighborhood water association has been around for many years, and if there are no complaints generated about the quality of the system. Mature neighborhood associations are unlikely to be challenged by Costa Rica providing that their wells are legally registered, they have a legal concession granted to withdraw a preapproved quantity of water, and they stick to pumping that amount of water or less.

Condominium Water System In this case, a well is registered duly to the condominium for the administration and distribution of water. Costa Rica will require the well within the condominium property to be legally registered, and will also require that the condominium is granted a concession to withdraw water from that well. To be clear, the seller needs to provide two forms of documentation: one proves legal registration of the well, and the other proves there is a concession for the use of its water.

ASADA (The best scenario for water rights.) An ASADA (Asociación Administradora del Acueducto y Alcantarillado) is a community organization bound by strict rules governing the creation and administration of all registered wells and concessions within the limits of the infrastructure of that ASADA.

An ASADA may or may not be entered into a Convenio de Delegación (which means a delegation contract with the National Water Association). Either way, an ASADA is a strong form of water rights. However, one that has entered into a Convenio de Delegación is the most desirable, as this is the most solid form of water rights a property can have in Costa Rica.

An ASADA must also be duly registered. ASADAs that have entered into a Convenio de Delegación have the full and legal right to substitute for the National Water Association as it relates to all matters concerning water generation and distribution for a community. It is the most solid form of water rights a property can have within Costa Rica. This is the water system we have in our community, Mar Vista.

What water documents do I need to obtain a building permit for a home?

You must provide two essential water documents before you are given a building permit from your local municipality. The first document is what is referred to as a Water Availability Letter. This letter is a prerequirement of the municipality before they will even consider granting you a building permit. The second document is the actual water hookup approval, which is granted once the property owner presents a fully stamped and certified building permit. This approval grants the user the right to purchase a water meter and to have unrestricted use of water.

Building in a foreign country is always a bit nerve-racking, but with the right information, there is a better chance things will go smoothly. Having honest and professional people on your side is critical, as is understanding the Costa Rican laws that affect your investment. Arming yourself with the above knowledge is the first step when house hunting in Costa Rica.

Happier Than A Billionaire

A compass has a magnetic field, turning one end of the needle north while pulling the other end south. It rests on a low-friction pivot point, and if held level, the needle oscillates until finally resting in its equilibrium position. Only then can you decide which way to go.

Our car had a compass on the dashboard, and to calibrate it, we had to drive in circles. The spinning was nauseating and never accurately set the device. That compass always pointed east, so I imagined we'd eventually end up in the Atlantic Ocean. Or maybe Tokyo. I suppose east is relative depending on where you're standing.

With GPS, there are few reasons to own a compass, but it's fun observing the wobbly dial, uncertain which way you're heading until the needle aligns with one coordinate. It must remain level to work, something I was not for most of my life. I spent years spinning in circles, pressing buttons, hoping to get pointed in the right direction.

I wished a portal would open in my office floor, one lit up with a swirling center. "Should I jump in? Am I brave enough to leave all this behind?" I'd ask myself. And one afternoon, when I couldn't take another day of doing the same thing I'd done the day before, I decided it was time. So with Rob, a cat, and a dog, we took a running start and hurled ourselves into the swirling center.

When you follow your dream, it's like jumping off a high dive at the community pool, one so high that your feet hit the bottom, and you kick as hard as you can to reach the surface again. Your lungs start to burn, and there's a moment of panic until you feel the water getting warmer. From here, it's just one more kick to fresh air. You can waste a lifetime standing on that high dive, too afraid of the cold water bottom to ever make it to the top.

Many of my readers have told me that they read my books in secret. Some have not yet told their bosses about retiring to Costa Rica; others don't want to hear people of no consequence chiming in with their opinions. "Why go there when you can live in Tampa?" a coworker might say. Thanks, Karen, but take no offense. You're not the one who should decide my fate.

Maybe you're a person who is simply looking for your mind to stop racing. To stop spinning in circles. I was searching for a quiet moment for most of my life. I found it in Costa Rica, where sea breezes taxied my anxiety away. The reprieve gave me time to reflect, to love, to forgive, and to dream about what was ahead. It encouraged me to pinpoint the quicksand of negativity and uncover the booby traps of criticism I held on to so tightly. Like loose change, it weighed me down. The only way to get rid of it was to turn myself upside down and let it spill from my pockets.

My happier life was not bought with money. I have lost a lot along the way. Happiness came when I stopped pretending that the small things didn't matter. When I stuck my bare feet in the grass and stared up at the stars, when I listened to rustling palm fronds and invited the ocean's undertow to pull on my ankles. And maybe that's where you find yourself today, questioning why the big things haven't made you happy. Why your mind keeps racing. Why you're still holding a compass, wondering which way to go.

Your magnetic pull may direct you toward the Caribbean coast or hurtle you into the Central Valley, living alongside a volcano or in a treehouse. But you can't get there without first leaping off the high dive.

Your compass needle will wobble along its pivot point, but once level, it'll find equilibrium— its one true coordinate. And from there, the warmer waters are just a few kicks away.

Rob said we'd be happier.
He was right.

About the Author

You made it this far! Congratulations. I suppose I should say something about myself. Preferably in third person. So here it goes.

Nadine Hays Pisani is the bestselling author of most things Costa Rican. She grew up near an Exxon refinery and now resides under a tree of howler monkeys.

She's married to Rob, who just disappeared into the backyard with a machete and an extension ladder.

Other Books by Nadine Hays Pisani

- Happier Than A Billionaire: Quitting My Job, Moving to Costa Rica, & Living the Zero Hour Work Week
- *Happier Than A Billionaire: The Sequel*
- *Happier Than A Billionaire: An Acre in Paradise*
- *The Costa Rica Escape Manual 2014*
- *The Costa Rica Escape Manual 2016*
- *The Costa Rica Escape Manual 2019*

Index

Made in the USA
San Bernardino, CA
15 January 2020